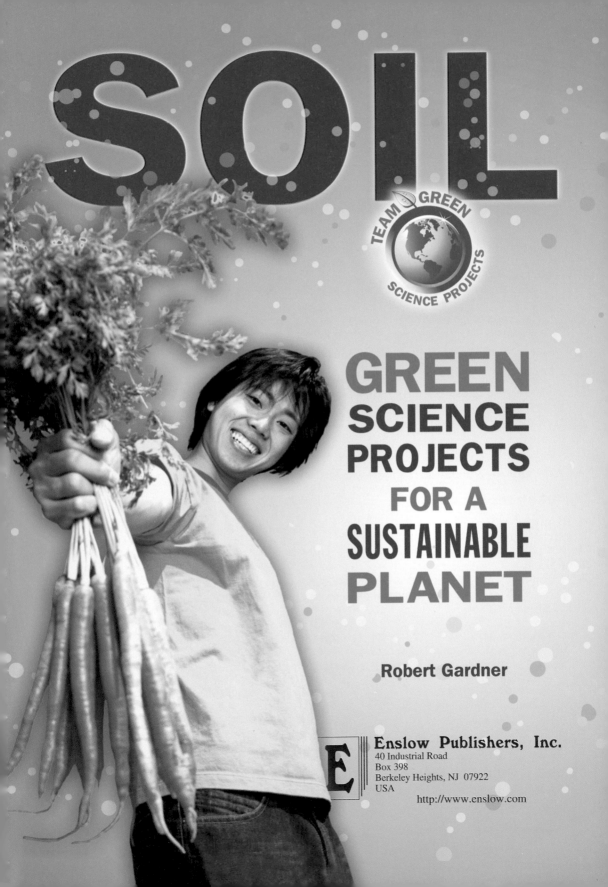

# SOIL

TEAM GREEN
SCIENCE PROJECTS

## GREEN
### SCIENCE
### PROJECTS
### FOR A
### SUSTAINABLE
### PLANET

**Robert Gardner**

**E**nslow Publishers, Inc.
40 Industrial Road
Box 398
Berkeley Heights, NJ 07922
USA

http://www.enslow.com

# SOIL

## GREEN Science Projects for a Sustainable PLANET

**Library of Congress Cataloging-in-Publication Data**

Gardner, Robert, 1929–
    Soil : green science projects for a sustainable planet / by Robert Gardner.
        p. cm. — (Team green science projects)
    Includes bibliographical references and index.
    Summary: "Provides environmentally friendly 'green' science projects about soil"—
        Provided by publisher.
    ISBN 978-0-7660-3647-5
    1. Soils—Juvenile literature. 2. Soils—Experiments—Juvenile literature. 3. Soil ecology—
        Juvenile literature. 4. Soil ecology—Experiments—Juvenile literature. 5. Science projects—
        Juvenile literature. I. Title.
    S591.3.G36 2011
    631.4078—dc22

                                                    2009043928

Printed in the United States of America

102010 Lake Book Manufacturing, Inc., Melrose Park, IL

10 9 8 7 6 5 4 3 2 1

**Illustration Credits:** Jacob Katari, p. 38; © 2010 Stephen Rountree (www.rountreegraphics.com), pp. 35, 42, 45, 56, 60, 74, 77, 80, 92, 95, 102, 118; Tom LaBaff and Stephanie LaBaff, pp. 30, 82 (b and c), 89.

**Photo Credits:** © 2010 Photos.com, a division of Getty Images. All rights reserved, p. 12; iStockphoto.com: © Abrieviljoen, p. 33, © Alex Fiodorov, p. 107, © Eric Michaud, p. 6, © Peter J Seager, p. 103; © Starfotograf, p. 119, © Stockphoto4u, p. 5; © Kenneth W. Fink/Photo Researchers, Inc., p. 16; Library of Congress, p. 99; © photolibrary.com, p. 1; Shutterstock.com, pp. 20, 27, 39, 66, 75, 82 (a), 85, 96, 106, 112, 122.

**Cover Photo:** © photolibrary.com

# Contents

 Indicates experiments that offer ideas for science fair projects.

Indicates experiments that offer ideas for science fair projects.

# Introduction

**S**oil is essential to our survival. Most of the plants we eat grow in soil. Soil is a remarkable combination of water and minerals that plants need to grow. It contains particles of sand, silt, clay, air, and water. It also has organic matter, such as decaying plant and animal tissues.

Global warming is causing climage changes that affect soil. Climates where certain crops thrived are no longer as productive because of higher temperatures. Climate changes have reduced rainfall in some regions. The soil has dried, and some has blown away. Other soils have been washed away by floods caused by excessive precipitation. Still more has been contaminated in various ways.

In this book, you will learn about soil. What is it made of? What are the effects of wind, rain, and agricultural activities on it? How can it be conserved to make a greener Earth? Much of what you learn will be accomplished through enjoyable experiments and other activities. They will also provide a better understanding of the scientific method.

At times, as you do the experiments, demonstrations, and other activities, you may need a partner to help you. It would be best to work with someone who likes experimenting as much as you do. In that way, you will both enjoy what you are doing. **If any safety issues or danger is involved in doing an experiment, you will be warned. In some cases, to avoid danger, you will be asked to work with an adult. Please do so.** We don't want you to take any chances that could lead to an injury.

# The Scientific Method

Scientists look at the world and try to understand how things work. They make careful observations and conduct research. Different areas of science use different approaches. Depending on the problem, one method is likely to be better than another. Designing a new medicine for heart disease, studying the spread of an invasive plant such as purple loosestrife, and finding evidence of water on Mars require different methods.

Despite the differences, all scientists use a similar general approach in doing experiments. It is called the scientific method. In most experimenting, some or all of the following steps are used: making an observation, formulating a question, making a hypothesis (an answer to the question) and a prediction (an if-then statement), designing and conducting an experiment, analyzing results and drawing conclusions about your prediction, and accepting or rejecting the hypothesis. Scientists then share their findings by writing articles that are published in journals.

You might wonder how to start an experiment. When you observe something in the world, you may become curious and ask a question. Your question, which could arise from an earlier experiment or from reading, may be answered by a well-designed investigation. Once you have a question, you can make a hypothesis. Your hypothesis is a possible answer to the question (what you think will happen). Once you have a hypothesis, it is time to design an experiment to test a consequence of your hypothesis.

In most cases you should do a controlled experiment. This means having two groups that are treated the same way except for the one thing being tested. That thing is called a variable. For example, suppose your question is "Do corn seeds germinate faster in sand than in garden soil?" Your hypothesis might be that seeds germinate faster in sand than in garden soil. You would use two groups of soils. One group, called the control group, would consist of corn seeds planted in garden soil. The other, the experimental group, would consist of corn seeds planted in sand. All the seeds and soils should be treated the same except for soil type. All seeds should be planted at the same depth, soils should receive the same amount of water and be kept at the same temperature, and so forth. Sandy soil is the variable. It is the difference between the two groups.

During the experiment, you should collect data. You would record the time between planting and the emergence of baby plants. By comparing the data collected from the control and experimental groups over a few days, you would draw conclusions.

Two other terms are often used in scientific experiments—*dependent* and *independent variables*. The dependent variable here is speed of seed germination, which was believed to be greater in sand. The independent variable is soil type. It doesn't depend on anything. After the data is collected, it is analyzed to see if it supports or rejects the hypothesis. The results of one experiment will often lead you to a related question. Or they may send you off in a different direction. Whatever the results, something can be learned from every experiment.

# Science Fairs

Some of the investigations in this book contain ideas that might lead you to a science fair project. Those project ideas are indicated with a symbol ( ). However, judges at science fairs do not reward projects or experiments that are simply copied from a book. For example, a diagram of a cross section of soil would not impress most judges; however, a unique method of separating soil particles according to size might gain their attention.

Science fair judges tend to reward creative thought and imagination. It is difficult to be creative or imaginative unless you are really interested in your project. Therefore, try to choose an investigation that excites you. And before you jump into a project, consider, too, your own talents and the cost of the materials you will need.

If you decide to use an experiment or idea found in this book for a science fair, find ways to modify or extend it. This should not be difficult. As you carry out investigations, new ideas will come to mind. You will think of questions that experiments can answer. The experiments will make excellent science fair projects, particularly because the ideas are your own and are interesting to you.

If you decide to enter a science fair and have never done so, read some of the books listed in the Further Reading section. These books deal specifically with science fairs. They provide plenty of helpful hints and useful information. The books will help you avoid the pitfalls that sometimes plague first-time entrants. You will learn how to prepare appealing reports that include charts and graphs, how to set up and display your work, how to present your project, and how to relate to judges and visitors.

# Your Notebook

Like any good scientist, you will find it useful to record your ideas, notes, data, and conclusions in a notebook. By doing so, you will be able to refer to things you have done. It will also help you in doing future projects. Your notebook should contain ideas you may have as you experiment, sketches you draw, calculations you make, and hypotheses you may suggest. It should include a description of every experiment you do, the data you record, and so on. It should also contain the results of your experiments, calculations, graphs you draw, and any conclusions you may be able to reach based on your results.

## Safety First

As with many activities, safety is important in science. Certain rules apply when doing experiments. Some of the rules below may seem obvious to you, but it is important that you follow all of them.

1. Have **an adult** help you whenever the book advises.

2. Wear eye protection and closed-toe shoes (not sandals). Tie back long hair.

3. Do not eat or drink while experimenting. Never taste substances being used (unless instructed to do so).

4. Do not touch chemicals.

5. The liquid in some thermometers is mercury (a dense liquid metal). It is dangerous to touch mercury or breathe mercury vapor, and such thermometers have been banned in many states. When doing these experiments, use only non-mercury thermometers, such as those filled with alcohol. If you have a mercury thermometer in the house, **ask an adult** if it can be taken to a local thermometer exchange location.

6. Do only those experiments that are described in the book or those that have been approved by **an adult**.

7. Maintain a serious attitude while conducting experiments. Never engage in horseplay or play practical jokes.

11

8. Before beginning an experiment, read all of the instructions carefully and be sure you understand them.

9. Remove all items not needed for the experiment from your work space.

10. At the end of every activity, clean all materials used and put them away. Then wash your hands thoroughly with soap and water.

# What Is Soil?

**S**oil (some call it dirt) covers nearly a third of Earth's surface. To farmers, it is the source of their livelihood—the medium in which their crops and pastures grow. To many homeowners, it is the matter that nourishes grass, trees, and bushes, and makes flowers bloom and gardens grow. Soil nurtures a greener Earth. Trees grow in soil, and they remove carbon dioxide, a greenhouse gas, from the air. By reducing the amount of carbon dioxide in the air, trees help to control global warming and climate change.

Soil is a mixture of tiny pieces of rock and decaying or decayed organic matter (dead plants and animals). It also contains air and water. The amount of organic matter varies, from zero in many desert soils to nearly 100 percent in some peats (carbon-rich decomposed plants). Healthy soils contain bacteria, fungi, various other microorganisms, and numerous small animals, such as earthworms. The organisms break down the organic matter, forming dark soil called humus. Humus is rich in nutrients. The nutrients, together with water and air, are essential for plant growth. This dark layer at the surface of soil may have a depth of several centimeters (inches) to half a meter (20 inches). Called topsoil, it is the soil farmers cultivate, the soil that nurtures plants. It takes thousands of years to form a thick layer of good topsoil. But, as you will see, it can quickly be lost if not properly cared for.

Beneath the dark topsoil, there are usually subsoils that lie between topsoil and solid bedrock. Subsoils are usually less dark because they lack organic matter. Their particles are generally larger than those found in topsoil. Above the solid bedrock are fragmented pieces of bedrock from which upper soil layers originated.

# 1.1 **Soil Layers**
## **(An Observation)**

Things **YOU** will **Need:**

✓ lawn or field
✓ shovel
✓ newspapers
✓ pen
✓ clear plastic bags
✓ notebook
✓ labels (masking tape will work)
✓ ruler or measuring tape

**1.** Obtain permission to dig a hole near the edge of a lawn, field, or woods.

**2.** First, examine the surface of the grass-covered soil. You may find litter (bits of leaves, twigs, and other debris) that will slowly become part of the organic matter in the soil below. What function might litter serve in its present location?

**3.** Using a shovel, remove the sod (grass-covered soil) from an area about 60 cm (2 ft) x 60 cm (2 ft). Place it on newspapers. Later, you will replace the sod.

**4.** On other newspapers, place the soil you continue to dig as you make a hole about 60 cm (2 ft) deep.

**5.** Look at the sides of the hole. Can you see layers in the soil? Do the layers have different colors? What is the color of the uppermost layer? In your notebook, make a sketch of any layers and record their colors.

6. Collect a sample of soil from each layer. Collect two samples from one of the layers. Be sure to include some of the soil from the grassy sod. Put the samples in clear plastic bags. Use tape and a pen to label the bag with the layer from which each sample came. You will use the samples in the next activity.

7. Shovel the soil back in the hole and replace the grassy sod.

A cut made through rocks and soil by road builders often reveals soil layers like the ones seen here.

# Soil Particles

The nonorganic particles of soil are tiny pieces of rocks produced by weathering. Weathering is the wearing away or dissolving of rocks. It can be caused by wind, freezing or moving water, friction, chemicals, or expansion and contraction caused by temperature changes. Soil particles made by the washing action of swift-flowing water tend to be round. Soil particles made in other ways are often angular with sharp edges and flat surfaces.

Soil particles are classified according to size. The largest particles are sand, which is mostly small pieces of quartz. Sand grains range in size from 0.06 to 2.0 millimeters in diameter. Particles intermediate in size are called silt. Silt particles are 0.002 to 0.06 millimeters in diameter. Clay has the smallest soil grains. They are less than 0.002 millimeters. Gravel, which consists of particles larger than 2.0 millimeters, is often found separately or, together with stones and rocks, mixed in with smaller soil particles.

Sand, as you probably know, feels gritty when rubbed between your fingers. Silt particles, which are best seen with a magnifying glass or microscope, feel like flour or talcum powder. Particles of clay, which are too small to be seen without a very good microscope, may feel sticky when wet.

Soils that are mostly clay hold water well and are rich in the nutrients that plants need. However, they are difficult to cultivate (prepare for planting), and can become waterlogged (saturated with water). Silty soils often lack nutrients and are easily washed away. Sandy soils are easy to work with. They drain well but lack nutrients.

# 1.2 **Separating Soil Particles**
## (An Experiment)

**Things YOU will Need:**

- sheets of paper
- soil samples collected in Section 1.1
- magnifying glass
- paper cup
- water
- tall, clear, quart jar with cover
- paper towel
- level surface
- spoon
- watch or clock

**K**nowing the relative size of sand, silt, and clay particles, which particles do you think are heaviest? Lightest?

Suppose you have soil that is a mixture of sand, silt, and clay. If you add water to a sample of such soil and shake the mixture, which soil particles will settle out first? Last? Form a hypothesis before you begin this experiment.

**1.** On separate sheets of paper, spread a small amount of soil from each of the soil samples you collected in Section 1.1. Use a magnifying glass to look at the soils. What do you see? Do some samples have more large particles than others? Can you find particles that look like grains of sand or pieces of rock? Can you find pieces of old plants—leaves, bark, roots, twigs, seeds, pine needles? Can you find any animals such as ants, beetles, grubs, or earthworms?

2. Pour one of the two soil samples you collected from one layer in Section 1.1 into a paper cup. Slowly add water to the cup. Do you see bubbles coming out of the soil? What was in the soil that accounts for the bubbles?

3. Thoroughly mix together the remaining samples you collected in Section 1.1.

4. Fill a tall, clear, quart jar about one-third of the way with the soil mixture. Then nearly fill the jar with water.

5. Put the cover on the jar. Shake the jar for one minute.

6. Put the jar on a folded paper towel on a level surface. Let the soil particles settle overnight.

Did anything in the soil samples float? If so, what do you think the floating pieces are?

Where are the biggest soil particles? The smallest? Was your hypothesis correct?

Some particles of clay are so small they may not settle out. They will remain suspended in the water, giving the water a cloudy appearance. Were there tiny clay particles in the soil you tested? How do you know?

## Ideas for Science Fair Projects

- Find a way to estimate what fraction of a soil sample is made up of sand, silt, or clay.

- What fraction of dry sand is actually air? Design and do an experiment to find out.

- Measure the depth of topsoil in different places. Where is it deepest? Least deep? Can you explain why?

# Sediments and Rivers

Rivers carve soil from their banks and carry it downstream. Much of that soil settles, especially when the water slows as the rivers empty into lakes or seas. These settled-out soils (sediments) reduce the depth of the water at the mouths of rivers. This can block the passage of ships entering or leaving the rivers. To prevent ships from getting stuck in the sediments, large dredging machines are often used to remove the soil.

This large machine is being used to dredge sediment from a harbor.

# 1.3 Where Does Soil Come From?
## (Demonstrations)

**Things YOU will Need:**

- safety glasses
- variety of small rocks with cracks or rough surfaces
- water
- plastic bottle with cap
- shallow plastic container about 7.5 cm (3 in) deep with tight-fitting cover
- freezer
- 2 small white or light-colored stones
- black construction paper
- 2 small dark-colored stones
- white paper
- soapless steel wool
- plastic lid
- glove

Soil particles come from rocks that have been dissolved or broken into small pieces. The process of making soil can occur in many different ways. Freezing is one way that rocks weather (break down) into soil. When water freezes, it expands. The expansion can split rocks or break off small pieces of them. These small rock particles mix with organic matter (rotting leaves, grass, bark, and other plant parts) to make soil. The rock particles contain the minerals that plants need to grow. The minerals dissolve in water in the soil and can then be taken up by plant roots.

SOIL

1. To see what happens to water when it freezes, fill a plastic bottle with water. Screw on the cap and put the bottle in a freezer overnight.

2. The next day remove the bottle. What has happened to the bottle? What happens to water when it freezes?

3. Find a variety of small rocks that have cracks or rough surfaces. Wash them off with water to remove any dirt that may be on them.

4. Put the rocks in a shallow plastic container that has a tight-fitting cover. Add water until all the rocks are under water. Then put the tight-fitting cover on the container.

5. Place the container in a freezer. Be sure it is level, so the rocks remain covered with water. Leave the container overnight while the water freezes.

6. Remove the container and take off the cover. Let the ice melt. Then examine the rocks. Do you see any small particles of rock in the water? If so, where do you think they came from?

7. Empty the water and any rock particles. Repeat the experiment several times with the same rocks. Each time look for small rock particles after the ice melts.

Roots growing into cracks in rocks can split the rock, releasing flakes that become soil. Falling rocks can collide with other rocks. Water in fast-flowing streams can cause stones to bang into one another. Let's see what falling rocks rubbing against stationary rocks can do.

8. **Put on safety glasses.** Find two small white or light-colored stones. Hold them over a sheet of black construction paper. Rub one stone against the other for about ten seconds. What do you find on the black paper?

9. **Put on safety glasses.** Find two small dark-colored stones. Hold them over a sheet of white paper. Rub one stone against the other for about ten seconds. What do you find on the paper?

The oxygen in air can react with minerals in rocks, forming oxides. For example, iron in some rocks will react with oxygen to form iron oxide (rust). Rocks can rust!

Lichens and mosses can grow on rocks. They produce chemicals that dissolve minerals in the rocks. The holes and cracks created by the chemical action can be filled with rain that freezes. Then pieces of rock split off and become part of the soil.

10. You can see how chemicals act on rocks. And you can do it at a faster rate than occurs in nature. Take a piece of soapless steel wool and soak it in water for a minute or two. Then put it on a plastic lid.

11. After several days, you will see that rust has formed on the steel. **Put on a glove** and tap the steel wool on a sheet of white paper. Can you see flakes of rust on the paper?

## Ideas for Science Fair Projects

- Design and do an experiment to show by what fraction water expands when it freezes.
- Do experiments to determine the density of water and ice. Use that information to confirm the percentage that water expands when it freezes.

# 1.4 Weathering of a "Rock"
## (A Demonstration)

**Things YOU will Need:**
- ✓ balance that can weigh to ± 0.1 gram
- ✓ dry bar of soap
- ✓ pen or pencil
- ✓ notebook
- ✓ sink and faucet
- ✓ clock or watch

As you know, soil is formed by the slow eroding of rocks due to weathering. Weathering is not limited to freezing water that breaks rocks apart. Water can also cause rocks to slowly weather away into tiny particles of soil. But weathering is a slow process. To speed up the process, you can drip water on a bar of soap to represent rain falling on a rock.

**1.** Weigh a dry bar of soap. Record the weight and the time.

**2.** Put the soap in a sink. Let a slow, steady drip, drip, drip from a faucet "rain" on the center of the bar of soap. Allow this slow erosion to go on for two hours.

**3.** While the erosion is taking place, count the number of drops of water that fall on the soap in one minute. Record that number.

**4.** After two hours, remove the bar of soap and let it dry.

**5.** When the soap is dry, reweigh it. How much soap eroded away? How many drops of water were required to produce the erosion? What is the rate of erosion in grams of soap per hour? What is the rate of erosion in grams of soap per liter of water? (It takes approximately 20,000 drops of water to fill a one-liter flask.)

## Ideas for Science Fair Projects

- Do an experiment to find out how the erosion of soap is affected by the speed at which the water drops strike the soap.

- Do an experiment to find out how the erosion of soap is affected by the rate at which the water drops strike the soap.

# 1.5 Soil From Chemical Weathering
## (A Demonstration)

Things **YOU** will **Need:**

- ☑ teaspoon
- ☑ baking soda
- ☑ large saucer
- ☑ medicine cup, measuring cup, or graduated cylinder
- ☑ white vinegar
- ☑ warm place

Soil can also form from chemical reactions. Acid rain and acids formed in soil can dissolve rocks. When the liquid evaporates, solid particles remain. To actually watch rocks weather chemically would be a centuries-long task. You can speed up the process as you did when you let a bar of soap represent a rock.

1. Place half a teaspoon of baking soda on a large saucer. The baking soda represents a rock.

2. Add about 50 mL (2 oz) of white vinegar. The vinegar represents acid rain or acidic soil water. You will see a chemical reaction occur. A similar reaction between acid rain and a rock might take years.

3. When the fizzing stops, check to be sure all the baking soda has disappeared. If some remains, add a little more vinegar.

**4.** Place the saucer in a warm place and let the liquid evaporate. This may take several days.

**5.** After the liquid evaporates, you will see bits of "soil" that formed when the liquid containing the dissolved "rock" evaporated.

**This statue has been damaged by acid rain.**

# 1.6 Rocks, Solids, and Temperature Change
## (A Demonstration)

**Things YOU will Need:**

- an adult
- hammer
- finishing nails
- 2 wooden blocks
- 2 tables
- ruler
- C-clamps
- copper wire
- metal washers
- rubber band
- pencil
- 2 friends
- 4 candles
- matches
- steel or iron wire
- Table 1

**Y**ou have seen that the expansion of water when it freezes can cause pieces of rock to break or flake off. Rocks themselves expand and contract with temperature changes. This also causes particles to break off. It is difficult to show the expansion of rocks, but most solids, including metals, expand when warmed. In this demonstration, you will show that a metal expands ever so slightly when heated.

**Ask an adult to help you with this experiment. You will be working with matches and candles.**

**1.** Hammer a finishing nail into one side of each of two wooden blocks. Then place two tables about 3 meters (10 ft) apart.

2. Fasten the blocks to the tables with C-clamps as shown in Figure 1a.

3. Put one end of a 3-meter (10-ft) length of copper wire through a metal washer. Wind the wire around itself several times to fasten it to the washer. Use a rubber band to

## Figure 1

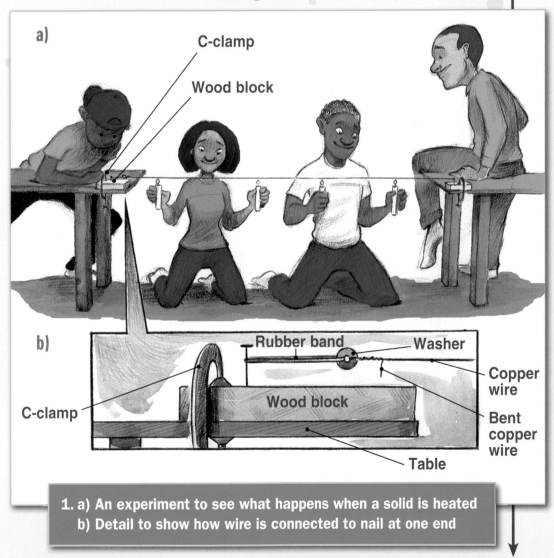

a)

C-clamp

Wood block

b)

Rubber band     Washer

Copper wire

C-clamp

Wood block

Bent copper wire

Table

1. a) An experiment to see what happens when a solid is heated
   b) Detail to show how wire is connected to nail at one end

attach the washer to the nail in the wooden block on the left, as shown in Figure 1b.

4. Bend the end of the wire so that it points straight down toward the block (Figure 1b). The bent end of the wire can serve as a pointer. Twist the other end of the long wire around the nail in the other block.

5. Pull the tables apart until the wire is nearly straight and the rubber band is stretched.

6. Use a pencil to mark the block directly under the end of the pointer.

7. **Under adult supervision**, ask two friends to slowly move the flames of four lighted candles back and forth along the wire while you watch the pointer.

8. When the pointer stops moving, mark the new position of the pointer. How much did the length of the wire change?

   Does the length of the long wire change when its temperature increases? How do you know? Does it get shorter as the temperature decreases?

9. **Under adult supervision**, repeat the experiment with a steel or iron wire of the same length. How did the change in length of the steel or iron wire compare with that of the copper wire?

Table 1 shows how much solids expand when a 1.0-meter length of the solid is heated through one degree Celsius. The table includes quartz, the source of sand grains.

# Ideas for Science Fair Projects

- Find a jar with a metal screw-on lid that is very tight. What can be done to make it easier to open the jar?

- Do experiments to show that thermometers and thermostats depend on the expansion of metals, liquids, or gases.

- What are some practical precautions that must be taken in construction concerning the way materials expand and contract with changes in temperature?

## Table 1:
### The increase in length of 1.00 meter of a number of different solids for each 1°C increase in temperature

| Solid | Increase in Length of 1.00 meter per 1°C | Solid | Increase in Length of 1.00 meter per 1°C |
|---|---|---|---|
| aluminum | 0.023 mm | iron | 0.012 mm |
| brass | 0.018 mm | platinum | 0.009 mm |
| copper | 0.017 mm | silver | 0.019 mm |
| glass (window) | 0.017 mm | quartz (source of sand) | 0.0004 mm |
| glass (Pyrex) | 0.003 mm | gold | 0.014 mm |

# 1.7 Are There Animals in Soil?
## (An Experiment)

✓ warm, damp, rich soil
✓ shovel
✓ newspaper
✓ plastic gloves
✓ magnifying glass
✓ guide book for small animals

You probably know that there are earthworms in soil. Rich garden soil may have as many as 500 earthworms per square meter. It is estimated that these animals ingest 18 tons of soil per acre in one year. They devour and digest microorganisms and dead plant tissue as they tunnel their way through soil. Their actions produce new soil, loosen existing soil, and provide openings for much needed water and air to reach the roots of plants.

Do you think there are other animals in soil? Form a hypothesis. Then do this experiment.

1. With the property owner's permission, dig up some warm, damp, rich soil. Place a shovelful on a newspaper and spread out the soil.

2. Put on a pair of plastic gloves and sift through the soil, searching for small animals. Use a magnifying glass to look for very small ones.

Did you find any earthworms? Did you see any other worms? How about arthropods such as insects, spiders, and other small segmented creatures?

**3.** Use a guide to small animals to see how many organisms you can identify. Table 2 lists some of the ones you might find in soil.

| Table 2: Some organisms and their numbers found in healthy agricultural soil. | |
| --- | --- |
| **Animals** | **Average number** |
| **Insects and their larvae** | **270 million/acre** |
| **Arthropods (centipedes, millipedes, beetles, spiders, crustaceans, etc.)** | **729 million/acre** |
| **Earthworms** | **0.73 million/acre** |
| **Bacteria** | **400 million/gram** |
| **Algae** | **0.1–0.8 million/gram** |

# 1.8 Making a Wormarium
## (An Observation)

Things **YOU** will **Need:**

- ✓ shovel
- ✓ topsoil
- ✓ earthworms
- ✓ large jar
- ✓ small jar with cap
- ✓ screen
- ✓ black construction paper
- ✓ sand
- ✓ scissors

To see earthworms in action, you can build a wormarium.

1. With the property owner's permission, dig up some rich soil and collect a few earthworms.

2. Place the worms in a wormarium like the one shown in Figure 2, which you can easily make.

3. Earthworms prefer to work in the dark, so make a collar and lid from black construction paper to cover the wormarium.

4. You can remove the dark covers for short periods of time to see what the worms are doing and have done. How do the worms react to the sudden presence of light?

5. To see how fast earthworms work, put a thin layer of sand on top of the dark soil. How long does it take the earthworms to cover up the layer of sand?

# Figure 2

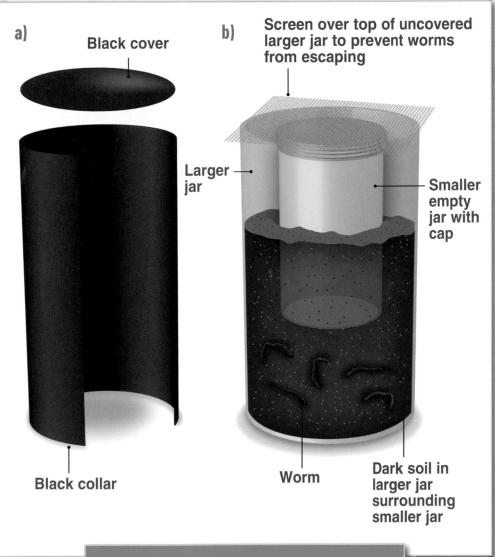

**a)** Black cover

Black collar

**b)** Screen over top of uncovered larger jar to prevent worms from escaping

Larger jar

Smaller empty jar with cap

Worm

Dark soil in larger jar surrounding smaller jar

A diagram of a wormarium you can build

# 1.9 Soil From Leaves
## (An Observation and an Experiment)

**Things YOU will Need:**
- ✓ wooded area
- ✓ shovel

If your home or school is near a wooded area, you can do some forest ground "archaeology."

1. With **adult permission**, go into a wooded area.

2. Clear the ground of any recently fallen leaves. Can you find some leaves that fell a year or two ago and have partially decomposed (broken down)?

3. Dig a little deeper. You will find pieces of leaves that fell several years ago.

4. Dig still deeper to reach the dark, rich soil (humus). It is made of the decomposed leaves that fell many years ago.

5. What do you think you will find if you dig below the humus? Make a hypothesis. Then dig. Was your hypothesis correct?

# Water and Soils

Plants need the nutrients in soil to grow. They also require water, and it is the water in soil that carries the nutrients to the roots of plants. Then it is absorbed and used in building new plant cells. Water is also needed for photosynthesis. During photosynthesis, plants combine water with carbon dioxide to make food for themselves.

When rain falls on the earth, some of it evaporates quickly. Some runs off into streams and rivers, which flow into ponds, lakes, or the ocean. Some is absorbed by leaves. The rest seeps into the ground, where it is called groundwater. The volume of Earth's groundwater is 60 times as great as the volume of water in all of Earth's lakes, ponds, rivers, and clouds.

As water sinks into the soil, it fills some of the spaces between the soil particles and rocks. At some depth, it completely fills all these spaces, saturating the soil with water. An aquifer is rocks or soil where water has saturated (filled) the spaces between the rocks and soil particles. The upper level of the saturated soil is called the water table. It is the top of an

## Figure 3

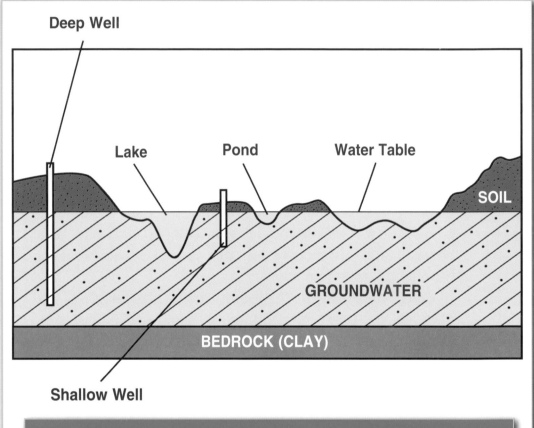

**Deep Well**

**Lake**  **Pond**  **Water Table**

**SOIL**

**GROUNDWATER**

**BEDROCK (CLAY)**

**Shallow Well**

A diagram of an aquifer (soil saturated with water), topsoil and subsoil, a pond indicating the water table (top of the aquifer), and a well from which water can be pumped from the aquifer

aquifer (see Figure 3). In some places where the water table is higher than the ground, it forms ponds, lakes, or swamps.

Aquifers provide underground reservoirs of water that serve as the source of water for many communities and farms. More than half the drinking water consumed in the United States comes from the ground. Two-thirds of the water added to soil to irrigate crops is pumped from aquifers. For an aquifer to be a stable source of water, it must be refilled by rain. If an aquifer is to remain stable, rainwater entering it must equal or exceed the water removed by pumping. Unfortunately, many aquifers are being refilled at a slower rate than they are being pumped. As a result, water tables are falling. Wells have to be drilled deeper, and the cost of pumping the water becomes greater.

# 2.1 Water-Holding Capacity of Different Soils
## (An Experiment)

**Things YOU will Need:**

- ☑ sand, gravel, potting soil, topsoil, clay-rich soil, garden soil
- ☑ cup
- ☑ newspapers
- ☑ warm, dry place
- ☑ can, such as a 6-ounce frozen juice can
- ☑ can opener
- ☑ coffee filters
- ☑ strong rubber band
- ☑ balance for weighing
- ☑ notebook
- ☑ pen or pencil
- ☑ container, such as an empty butter tub
- ☑ water

For plants to grow in soil, the soil must hold water between its particles. Based on what you know about soils from Chapter 1, which type of soil do you think will hold the most water per gram of soil? Which will hold the least amount of water per gram of soil? Form a hypothesis. To see if your hypothesis is correct, you can do an experiment.

1. Collect soils made up of different particle sizes, such as sand, potting soil, topsoil, clay-rich soil, and garden soil, as well as gravel.

2. Put a cup of each soil sample on separate sheets of newspaper. Spread the soils across the paper. Let them dry in a warm place for a week.

3. Remove the top and bottom of a can, such as a 6-ounce frozen juice can.

4. Cover one end of the can with a coffee filter. Use a strong rubber band to fasten it securely to the can, as shown in Figure 4.

5. Weigh the empty can and record its mass.

6. Prepare a data table like the one below.

| Type of soil | Mass of dry soil (g) | Mass of wet soil (g) | Mass of water in wet soil (g) | Mass of water absorbed per gram of dry soil (g) |
|---|---|---|---|---|

7. Add one type of soil to the can until it is about three-quarters full. Record the type of soil in your data table.

8. Weigh the can of dry soil. How can you find the mass of the soil in the can? Record that mass in your data table.

9. Hold the can over an empty container. Slowly pour water from a cup onto the soil. When water begins to drip through the soil into the container below, stop adding water. When water stops dripping from the can, assume the soil holds as much water as it can.

10. Weigh the can of wet soil. Record the mass of the wet soil in your data table.

11. Calculate the mass of water in the saturated soil. Record that mass in your data table.

## Figure 4

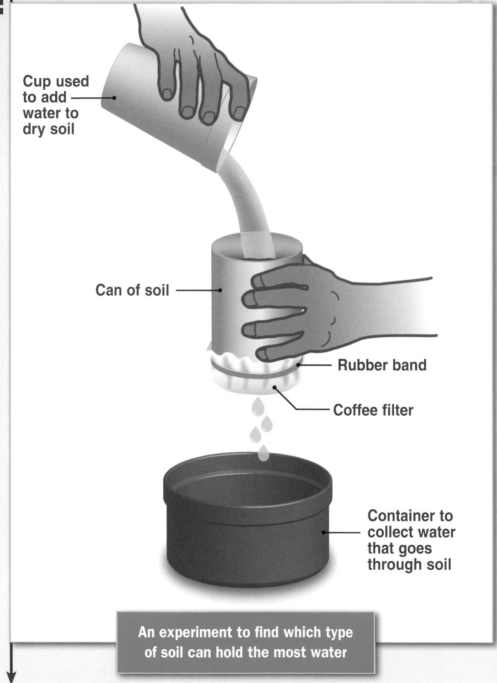

Cup used to add water to dry soil

Can of soil

Rubber band

Coffee filter

Container to collect water that goes through soil

**An experiment to find which type of soil can hold the most water**

**12.** Calculate and record the mass of water absorbed per gram of the dry soil. Record that mass per gram in your data table.

For example, suppose the dry soil weighed 100 grams and the wet soil weighed 150 grams. The mass of water in the saturated soil was 150 g – 100 g = 50 g. The mass of water absorbed per gram of dry soil was

$$\frac{50 \text{ g}}{100 \text{ g}} = 0.5 \text{ g of water/g of dry soil.}$$

**13.** Empty the can of wet soil. Wash and dry the can.

**14.** Repeat the experiment for each type of soil.

Was your hypothesis correct?

Save your dry samples for Experiment 2.2.

# 2.2 Reaching the Aquifer: Permeability
## (An Experiment)

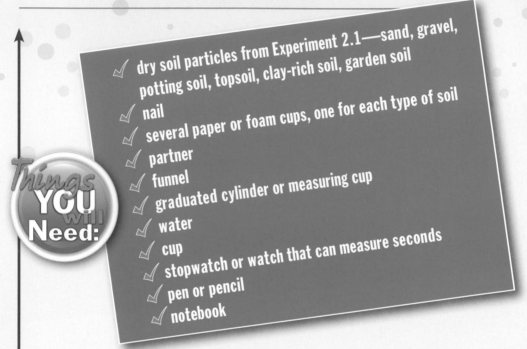

**Things YOU will Need:**

- ☑ dry soil particles from Experiment 2.1—sand, gravel, potting soil, topsoil, clay-rich soil, garden soil
- ☑ nail
- ☑ several paper or foam cups, one for each type of soil
- ☑ partner
- ☑ funnel
- ☑ graduated cylinder or measuring cup
- ☑ water
- ☑ cup
- ☑ stopwatch or watch that can measure seconds
- ☑ pen or pencil
- ☑ notebook

For rainwater to reach the aquifer, it must permeate (move through) the soil above the water table. How fast the water travels through the soil depends on the soil's permeability. You can test the permeability of different soils. Which type of soil do you think will be the most permeable? Make a hypothesis. Then do this experiment.

1. Use a nail to punch holes in the bottoms of several paper or foam cups. You will need one cup for each type of soil. Punch the holes from the inside of the cup.

2. Fill the cups two-thirds of the way with different dry soils. You could put sand in one, gravel in another, clay-rich soil in a third, garden or potting soil in a fourth, etc.

3. Have a partner hold one cup of soil above a funnel that rests on a graduated cylinder or measuring cup, as shown in Figure 5.

## Figure 5

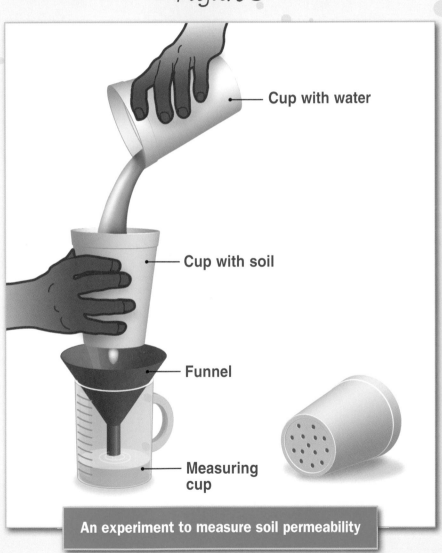

Cup with water

Cup with soil

Funnel

Measuring cup

**An experiment to measure soil permeability**

**4.** Ask your partner to slowly pour two-thirds of a cup of water (more if needed) onto the soil. Start timing.

**5.** Watch the water level in the graduated cylinder or measuring cup. Record the volume of water that passes through the soil in 10 seconds, 20 seconds, 30 seconds, and so on until the water stops passing through the soil.

**6.** Repeat the experiment for each type of soil.

Which type of soil was the most permeable? Which soil was the least permeable? Was your hypothesis correct?

# 2.3 The Space Between Soil Particles: Porosity (An Experiment)

**Things YOU will Need:**

- cup
- sand
- flat pan or cookie sheet
- sun, a 120°F oven, or a heat lamp
- large sheet of paper
- graduated cylinder or metric measuring cup
- plastic or foam cup
- water
- pen or pencil
- notebook

**P**articles of soil are solid, but the spaces between the particles are filled with air or water. What fraction of a volume of dry sand do you think is actually air? Form a hypothesis. Then do this experiment, for which you will need **dry sand**. (Wet or damp sand would have water between at least some of the particles.)

1. Pour about a cup of sand onto a flat, oven-safe pan, such as a cookie sheet. Dry the sand using the sun, a 120°F oven, or a heat lamp.

2. Fold a large sheet of paper in half. When the sand is thoroughly dry, open the paper and empty the cooled pan of sand into the fold. The folded paper will allow you to pour the dry sand neatly.

3. Use the paper to pour the sand into a graduated cylinder or metric measuring cup. Add sand until the cylinder or cup is about two-thirds full. Record the volume of the sand. Remember that part of the volume is the air between the sand particles.

4. Now pour the dry sand into a plastic or foam cup.

5. Add water to the graduated cylinder or metric measuring cup until it is about one-third full. Record the volume of the water.

6. Slowly pour the sand from the cup into the water in the graduated cylinder or measuring cup. The water will displace the air and fill the spaces between the sand particles. Record the new volume—the volume of the sand and water.

7. What percentage of dry sand is actually occupied by air? What percentage is made up of sand particles?

Suppose the volume of dry sand was 70 cm³ (70 mL). When the dry sand was added to 33 cm³ of water, the total volume became 75 cm³. The volume of the dry sand grains alone must have been:

volume of sand and water together − volume of water alone = volume of sand, so

**75 cm³ − 33 cm³ = 42 cm³.**

Volume of air in the sand = volume of dry sand with air − volume of sand without air, so

**70 cm³ − 42 cm³ = 28 cm³.**

Now those spaces are filled with water; therefore, the percentage of the space occupied by water, previously air, is:

$$\frac{28 \text{ cm}^3}{70 \text{ cm}^3} = 0.40 = 40\%$$

## Idea for a Science Fair Project

Does the shape of the particles affect the amount of space between the particles? Design and do experiments to find out.

# 2.4 Particle Size and the Space Between (An Experiment)

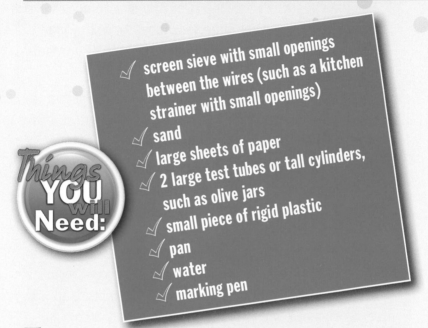

**Things YOU will Need:**

- ☑ screen sieve with small openings between the wires (such as a kitchen strainer with small openings)
- ☑ sand
- ☑ large sheets of paper
- ☑ 2 large test tubes or tall cylinders, such as olive jars
- ☑ small piece of rigid plastic
- ☑ pan
- ☑ water
- ☑ marking pen

**F**orm a hypothesis to answer this question: Does particle size affect the amount of space between the particles? Then do the following experiment.

1. Find a screen sieve with small openings between the wires. A kitchen strainer with small openings will probably work well.

2. Obtain some sand. Sand usually contains a mixture of coarse sand (large particles) and fine sand (small particles).

3. Fold two large sheets of paper in half to make a crease. Unfold them.

4. Sift some sand through the sieve to separate large particles from small ones. Let the small particles fall onto one piece of paper. The larger particles will remain on the sieve.

5. Empty the large particles onto the second piece of paper.

6. Use the papers to empty the large and small particles into separate but identical large test tubes or tall cylinders, such as olive jars. Label the tubes "L" and "S" for large and small particles.

7. Tap the tubes to make the particles pack together as tightly as possible. Add more particles as the grains pack together until both tubes are full.

8. Cover one of the tubes with a small piece of rigid plastic. Hold the cover tightly against the tube as you invert it and place it in a pan of water. When the mouth of the tube is under the water (but not touching the bottom), remove the cover. The sand particles will fall into the pan as they are replaced by water. The air between the particles, which is less dense than water, will remain in the tube. Mark the level of water in the inverted tube with a marking pen.

9. Repeat the process for the other tube.

What do you conclude? Does particle size affect the amount of space between the particles?

## Idea for a Science Fair Project

Assume all the particles are spheres. Use diagrams and your knowledge of the volumes of cubes and spheres to explain the conclusion you reached in Experiment 2.4.

# 2.5 Percolation and Particle Size
## (An Experiment)

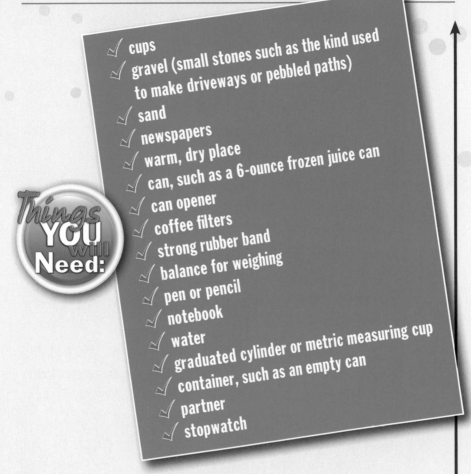

**Things YOU will Need:**

- ☑ cups
- ☑ gravel (small stones such as the kind used to make driveways or pebbled paths)
- ☑ sand
- ☑ newspapers
- ☑ warm, dry place
- ☑ can, such as a 6-ounce frozen juice can
- ☑ can opener
- ☑ coffee filters
- ☑ strong rubber band
- ☑ balance for weighing
- ☑ pen or pencil
- ☑ notebook
- ☑ water
- ☑ graduated cylinder or metric measuring cup
- ☑ container, such as an empty can
- ☑ partner
- ☑ stopwatch

For gardens and other agricultural areas, it is important that their soils be able to hold water, because plants need water to grow. However, there are places where it is wise to have soils that drain quickly and well.

The passage of water through soil is called percolation. Soils that allow water to percolate quickly are called permeable. They are used under the sod of many athletic fields. It is important to have outdoor games such as baseball and tennis played on a dry surface. Percolation is also a critical factor in building wastewater systems, highways, and other places where good drainage is needed.

Based on what you know about soil, how would you expect the size of the soil particles to affect percolation? Develop a hypothesis to answer this question. Then check your hypothesis by doing this experiment.

1. Collect a cupful of gravel—small stones such as the kind used to make driveways or pebbled paths. Also collect a cupful of some sand, which consists of smaller particles.

2. Spread the stones and sand on separate pieces of newspaper. Let them dry in a warm place for a week.

3. Remove the top and bottom of a can, such as a 6-ounce frozen juice can.

4. Cover one end of the can with a coffee filter. Use a strong rubber band to fasten it securely to the can, as you did in Experiment 2.1. Use a balance to weigh the can. Record the mass of the can in your notebook.

5. Nearly fill the can with the small stones. Weigh the can and stones and record their mass.

6. Add 100 mL of water to a graduated cylinder or metric measuring cup.

7. Hold the can of stones over a container such as an empty tin can. Pour the 100 mL of water into the can of stones. At the same time, have a partner start a stopwatch.

8. Let water percolating through the stones collect in the container beneath the can of stones. When no more water comes through the stones, have your partner stop the watch.

9. Reweigh the can of stones. How much water remains in the stones? What volume of water percolated through the stones? How long did it take for the water to percolate through the soil particles?

10. Empty the stones from the can. Rinse and dry the can.

11. Repeat the experiment using an equal volume of dry sand.

How much water remains in the sand? What volume of water percolated through the sand? How long did it take? Was your hypothesis correct?

## Idea for a Science Fair Project

At a garden supply store, obtain different types of soil—soils rich in clay, silt, or sand, and potting soil. Test the different soils for their water holding capacity and for percolation.

## Water, Plants, and Soils

Soils that contain a lot of clay hold water very well. Sand and gravel do not hold water well, but they provide good drainage because water readily flows through them. Potting soil, topsoil, and garden soil hold water and allow plants to grow. How much they hold depends on the percentage of clay they contain. Soil that is good for growing plants is about 25 percent clay. Too much clay can cause soil to become so wet that air cannot reach the plants' roots. The root cells need oxygen to survive. The percentages of different soil particles in good agricultural soil (loam) are about 17% coarse sand, 30% fine sand, 23% clay, and 30% silt.

# 2.6 Water and Capillarity
## (An Experiment)

Things YOU will Need:

- ✓ water
- ✓ food coloring
- ✓ shallow dish
- ✓ 2 small drinking glasses
- ✓ glass tubes with different diameters (borrow from a science lab)
- ✓ paper towel
- ✓ magnifying glass
- ✓ tape
- ✓ scissors
- ✓ ruler

**W**ater adheres (sticks) to glass and other solids because there is an attraction between water molecules and the molecules of the solids. Water is also cohesive: it holds together very well. Hypothesis: Because water holds together very well and adheres to glass and many other substances, it will "climb up" glass tubes and other surfaces. To test this hypothesis, you can do an experiment.

1. Add some water and a few drops of food coloring to a shallow dish.

2. Invert two small drinking glasses and place them in the colored water.

# Figure 6

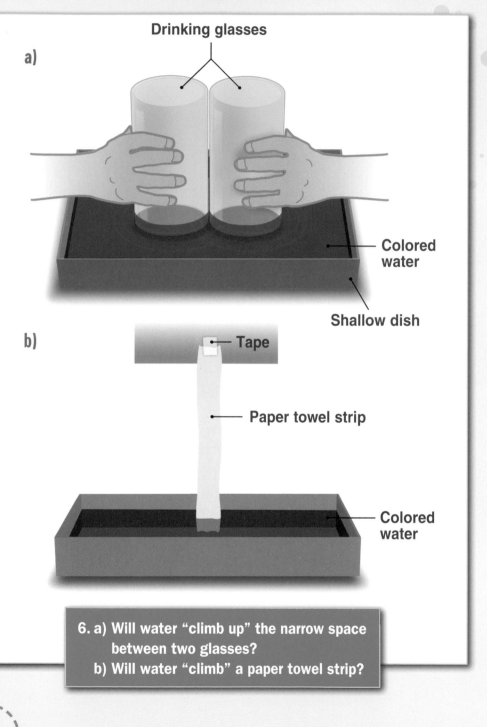

**a)**

Drinking glasses

Colored water

Shallow dish

**b)**

Tape

Paper towel strip

Colored water

6. a) Will water "climb up" the narrow space between two glasses?
   b) Will water "climb" a paper towel strip?

**3.** Move the sides of the glasses very close together, as shown in Figure 6a. What happens to the water in the narrow space between the glasses?

**4.** If possible, borrow some glass tubes with different diameters from a science lab. Place the tubes upside down in some colored water. How does the diameter of the tube affect the height to which the water rises inside the tube?

**5.** Tear off a small piece of a paper towel. Use a magnifying glass to examine the piece of towel. Can you see the tiny wood fibers that make up the towel? Are there narrow spaces between the wood fibers? Will water "climb up" paper towels?

**6.** To find out, cut a strip about 2.5 cm (1 in) wide from a paper towel. Find something to which you can tape the top of the strip so that it hangs vertically. Put the lower end of the towel into a shallow dish of colored water (see Figure 6b). Does water "climb up" the towel? Was the hypothesis correct?

The tendency of water and some other liquids to "climb up" narrow tubes and spaces is called capillarity.

# Ideas for Science Fair Projects

- Design and carry out an experiment to show that the height that water rises in a tube is inversely proportional to the diameter of the tube. In other words, show that doubling the diameter halves the height of the water, tripling the diameter reduces the height to a third, and so on.

- Cut long strips of paper towels that have different widths. Does the width of the strip affect the height to which water will ascend within the towel? If it does, how can you explain what you observe?

- Find a way to enclose the paper towel strips. You might use long, wide plastic tubes or make covers from plastic wrap or waxed paper. Does enclosing the strips affect the height to which the water will rise? If so, can you explain why?

# 2.7 Water, Soil, and Capillarity
## (An Experiment)

You know that gravity pulls water downward in soil. But you also know that there are small spaces between soil particles, just as there are small spaces between the wood fibers in paper towels. Do you think capillarity can cause water to move upward in soil? Form a hypothesis. Then try the following experiment.

1. Find a clear, rigid, plastic cup. **Ask an adult** to cut away the bottom of the cup with a sharp knife.

2. Cover the bottom of the cup with a coffee filter. Use a strong rubber band to hold the filter in place as you did with the can in Experiment 2.1.

3. Add some water to a shallow dish. Put a few drops of food coloring in the water and stir. The food coloring will make the water easier to see in soil.

**4.** Carefully fill the cup with fine, dry sand. Put the cup of sand in the shallow colored water as shown in Figure 7. Watch for a few minutes to see if the colored water moves upward in the sand. If it does, how high will it rise? Was your hypothesis correct?

## Figure 7

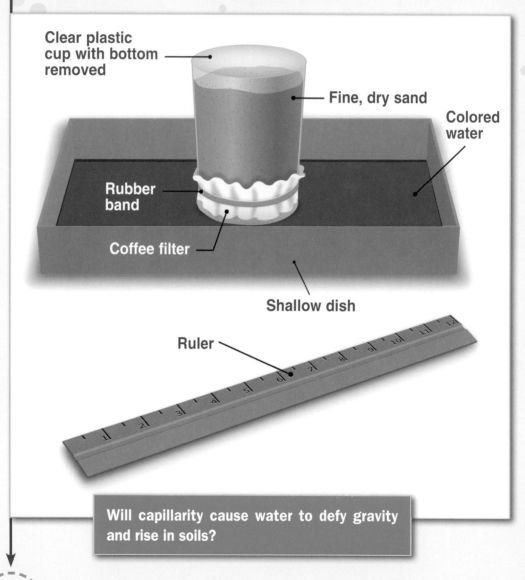

Clear plastic cup with bottom removed

Fine, dry sand

Colored water

Rubber band

Coffee filter

Shallow dish

Ruler

Will capillarity cause water to defy gravity and rise in soils?

## Idea for a Science Fair Project

In which type of soil will capillarity cause water to rise highest? Form a hypothesis. Then repeat Experiment 2.7 using different soils—those rich in clay or silt, coarse sand, potting soil, etc. Was your hypothesis correct? (If the water climbs to the top of the cup, you will have to use taller containers that allow you to see the water in the soil "climb" to greater heights.)

# 2.8 In Which Soils Do Plants Grow Best?
## (An Experiment)

**Things YOU will Need:**

- small flower pots
- soils—sand, gravel, garden soil, potting soil, and others
- large bean seeds, such as lima bean seeds
- warm, sunny place
- water
- ruler
- notebook and pen or pencil

**D**o you think plants will grow better in some soils than in others? Form a hypothesis. Then do this experiment.

1. Nearly fill several small flower pots with different soils. Use sand, gravel, garden soil, potting soil, topsoil, and other soils you may have.

2. In each soil, plant two or three large bean seeds about an inch deep.

3. Put all the pots in a warm sunny place. Keep the soils damp, not wet. The only variable should be the soil. All other conditions should be identical.

After a few days, the germinating seeds will push through the soil and the plants will begin to grow.

**4.** Measure the heights of all the plants each day with a ruler. Keep a record of their growth and the soil in which they are growing. Also record the appearance of the young plants. Do you see any differences among them? For example, do plants in some soils tend to develop yellowish leaves instead of green?

In which soil did plants grow best? In which soil was growth poorest?

# 2.9 Will Seeds Germinate Without Soil? (An Experiment)

**Things YOU will Need:**
- ✓ paper towels
- ✓ plastic container
- ✓ water
- ✓ bean seeds
- ✓ cardboard

**W**ill seeds germinate in the absence of soil? Form a hypothesis. Then do this experiment.

1. Place several damp paper towels in a plastic container. Put a few bean seeds on the towels.

2. Cover the seeds with more damp towels. Then place a sheet of cardboard on the container to reduce evaporation.

3. Keep the towels damp, not wet. Look at the seeds and check the towels several times each day to be sure they are damp. Do the seeds germinate? If they do, will they continue to grow without soil?

What do you conclude? Do seeds need soil to germinate? If not, what do they need?

## Ideas for Science Fair Projects

- Given adequate water and soil, how do light and temperature affect the growth of plants? Do experiments to find out.

- Does the color of the light reaching a green plant affect its growth? Do experiments to find out.

# Seeds, Soil, and Germination

As you have seen, seeds can germinate without soil. There is food stored in the seeds that provides the energy the plant embryos need to germinate and begin to grow. Once they break through the soil, green plants can make their own food. They need only light, water, warmth, the right minerals from the soil, and carbon dioxide that enters through their leaves. The process by which they make food is called photosynthesis. During photosynthesis, carbon dioxide and water are combined to make sugar. The process requires a catalyst, a substance that makes the process go faster. The catalyst is chlorophyll, the pigment found in green plants that gives them their color. Light provides the energy that is stored in the sugar.

# Hydroponics

Plants can actually grow to maturity without soil. They will grow in water as long as the water contains the dissolved minerals normally found in soil. Growing plants in this manner is called hydroponics. You may find hydroponically grown vegetables, especially lettuce, in some food markets.

There are advantages to growing plants without soil. (1) The concentrations of nutrients in the water can be controlled precisely. This allows plants to absorb the specific nutrients they are known to need in concentrations most suitable for growth. (2) The conditions in hydroponic solutions are unfavorable for the growth of bacteria, fungi, and other disease-causing organisms. (3) The hydroponic liquid can be circulated and aerated. This ensures that oxygen will be available to root cells. (4) There are no weeds to compete with the plants. (5) No tilling is required.

However, it is unlikely that hydroponics will ever replace soil as the common way to grow vegetables and flowers. Although its products are often superior to those grown in soil, hydroponic gardening requires expensive equipment and skilled workers. Consequently, hydroponically grown products generally cost more than those grown in soil.

**These plants are growing in water enriched with minerals the plants need to grow.**

# 2.10 Soil pH
## (A Measurement)

**Things YOU will Need:**

- ✓ soil from garden, flower bed, or lawn
- ✓ plastic jar
- ✓ water
- ✓ tweezers
- ✓ pH paper with chart showing color for various pH values
- ✓ watch or clock

**S**oils may be acidic, alkaline (basic), or neutral. Acids are chemicals that release hydrogen ions ($H^+$) in water. Hydrogen ions are hydrogen atoms that have lost their electron. An acid's strength depends on its concentration of hydrogen ions in water.

A strong acid is hydrochloric acid. It is a compound of hydrogen and chlorine. Molecules of hydrogen chloride (HCl) ionize (change to ions) in water and become hydrogen ions ($H^+$) and chloride ions ($Cl^-$). The reaction can be shown using a chemical equation:

$$HCl \rightarrow H^+ + Cl^-$$

Bases form hydroxide ions ($OH^-$) in water. For example, sodium hydroxide (NaOH), also known as lye, is made up of sodium ions ($Na^+$) and hydroxide ions. These ions separate in water, as shown by the following equation:

$$NaOH \rightarrow Na^+ + OH^-$$

The strength of an acid or base can be determined by its concentration of hydrogen ions. This concentration is measured as pH. Substances with a pH less than 7 are acidic; substances with a pH greater than 7 are basic (alkaline); substances with a pH of 7 are neutral. Very acidic soil has a pH of 3 to 5. A soil with a pH of 8 to 10 is mildly basic (alkaline) according to chemists, but is very basic for plants. In fact, most plants don't do well in soils with a pH greater than 8.

Litmus paper can determine whether a substance is an acid or a base, but it cannot measure pH. However, there are acid-base indicators that change color at different concentrations of hydrogen ions. Several such indicators are blended in pH paper, which can be used to measure the entire pH range from 1 to 14.

1. To find the pH of soil in your garden, flower bed, or lawn, fill a jar about one-third of the way with the soil to be tested. Add water until the jar is about two-thirds full.

2. Put the cover on the jar and shake vigorously to mix the soil and water thoroughly.

3. Let the soil settle for five minutes.

4. Use tweezers to hold one end of a piece of pH paper. Dip the other end into the soil solution.

5. Compare the color of the wet pH paper with the color chart on the pH paper roll or container. What is the pH of the soil you tested?

# Ideas for Science Fair Projects

- Investigate other acid-base indicators. Indicators can be found in many school science rooms or obtained from a science supply company (see Appendix). These include phenolphthalein, methyl orange, methyl red, bromthymol blue, congo red, indigo carmine, and alizarin yellow. Other than color, how do they differ?

- Prepare a cup of tea. Add a few drops of lemon juice, which is acidic. What evidence do you have that tea is a natural acid-base indicator?

- Vinegar is acidic and ammonia water is basic. **Under adult supervision**, use these two liquids to see if unsweetened grape juice and an extract of red cabbage leaves boiled in water are acid-base indicators.

- See if you can extract dyes from garden flowers. How do these colors respond to acids and bases? Are they acid-base indicators?

## Soil pH and Plants

If you see a forest of conifers, such as pines and firs, you know the soil is acidic and probably sandy. The same is true of heathers. Other plants, such as many that grow on grassland, prefer an alkaline soil.

The plants shown in Table 3 grow in a pH range from 4 to 8 (from mildly acidic to slightly alkaline).

Some plants are natural pH indicators. Mophead hydrangeas, for example, are blue in soil with a pH of

5.0 to 5.6, the pH of ordinary rain. They are pink in soil that has a pH of 6.0 or more. To make such hydrangeas more distinctly blue, you can add aluminum sulfate [$Al_2(SO_4)_3$]. To make them pinker, you can reduce the soil's acidity ("sweeten" it) by adding lime.

## Table 3:
### The best soil pH for a number of plants

| pH of 4–5 | pH of 5–6 | pH of 6 | pH of 7 | pH of 7–8 |
|---|---|---|---|---|
| Azaleas | Potatoes | Citrus fruits | Alfalfa | Cabbage |
| Rhododendron | Grapes | Ferns | Clover | Beets |
| Blueberries | Parsnips | Peppers | Asparagus | Carrots |
| Cranberries | Barley | Squash | Watermelon | Celery |
| Holly | Tomatoes | Beans | Cucumber | Lettuce |

Plants, like humans and other animals, require certain elements in order to live. Some of the important elements they need are listed here.

- *Magnesium* is one of the elements in chlorophyll. A low concentration of magnesium ions ($Mg^{++}$) in soil reduces chlorophyll production. This causes plants to develop a pale greenish-yellow color, a condition called chlorosis.

- *Nitrogen* is required by plants in larger amounts than any other element. It is found in all proteins, chlorophyll, and other organic compounds. Plant growth in nitrogen-deficient soil is stunted. The plants are unable to make enough protein;

they often do not flower; and if they do flower, their seeds and fruit are tiny.

- *Sulfur*, like nitrogen, is found in most proteins. Since proteins are a vital part of cell structure, plants growing in sulfur-deficient soil show the same symptoms as those lacking enough nitrogen.

- *Phosphorus* is another element found in proteins. Lack of this element retards growth and hinders cell division.

- *Calcium* is needed to build cell walls, control the movement of certain chemicals across cell membranes, and promote the absorption of water. It combines with some organic acids, which prevents their accumulation in cells. Lack of calcium stunts root growth and causes a general weakening of the plant.

- *Potassium* is involved in regulating a number of processes, including photosynthesis, that go on in living plant cells. Plants lacking sufficient potassium may have weak stems, shriveled seeds, grow poorly, and often show leaf discoloration.

- *Iron* is needed to make chlorophyll. Consequently, plants in iron-deficient soil do not grow well.

- *Boron, manganese, zinc,* and *copper* ions are required for healthy plant growth but only in small amounts. These ions regulate certain vital chemical reactions in plant cells.

# Soil Erosion

Earth's soil is being slowly washed into the oceans. The process is called erosion, and you can see it happening. Water, ice, wind, and gravity are moving soil downhill to the seas. Erosion is slow but measurable. A large mountain in Colorado, Pikes Peak, is shrinking by 30 cm (12 in) every thousand years. At that rate, in 9 million years the 14,000-foot-tall mountain will be flat.

You may think 9 million years is a long time, but to a geologist it is not long at all. Earth is estimated to be 4.5 billion years old, so 9 million years is only 0.2 percent of Earth's life to date. It would be equivalent to about 73 days in a human life that spanned one century, or less than three minutes of a 24-hour (1,440-minute) day.

Over millions of years, mountains erode away as volcanoes and upheavals create new ones. But on a scale of years and decades, advocates of a greener Earth must be concerned with the erosion of soil. It is needed to grow the food we will eat tomorrow and for years to come.

# 3.1 Soil Erosion by Rain
## (An Experiment)

Things **YOU** will **Need:**

- ☑ dry sand
- ☑ large, shallow pan or tray
- ☑ eyedropper
- ☑ water
- ☑ meterstick or yardstick
- ☑ different types of soil—clay soil, potting soil, garden soil, gravel

**D**o you think raindrops can cause soil to erode? Form a hypothesis. Then do this experiment.

1. Place a thin layer of dry sand on a large, shallow pan or tray.

2. Use an eyedropper to make drops of water ("rain") fall on the soil from different heights. You might let the drops fall from heights of 10 cm (4 in), 20 cm (8 in), 40 cm (16 in), and 1.0 meter (1 yd). How does the soil respond to different drop heights?

3. To provide wind-blown rain, move the eyedropper horizontally across the soil at different heights (see Figure 8a). Is the effect of wind-blown rain different?

4. Raise one end of the pan or tray to simulate sloped land (see Figure 8b). Describe how the impact of raindrops falling on sloped land differs from that of rain falling on flat ground.

## Figure 8

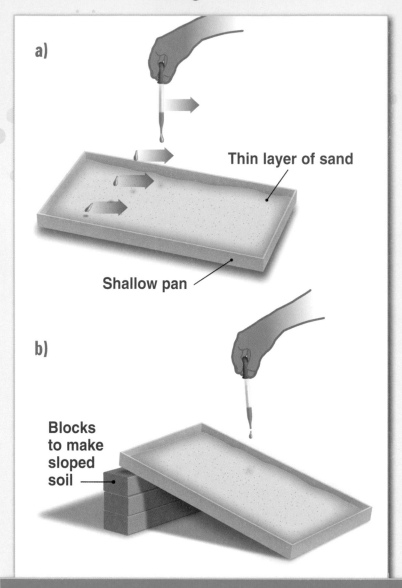

a)

Thin layer of sand

Shallow pan

b)

Blocks to make sloped soil

8. a) To simulate wind-driven rain, move the eyedropper horizontally as you squeeze out drops.
   b) Raise one end of the tray to simulate rain falling on sloped land.

**5.** Add enough water to make the sand wet (not soaking). How does the effect of raindrops on wet soil differ from their effect on dry soil?

**6.** Repeat the experiment with different types of soil. You might try clay soil, potting soil, garden soil, and gravel. Do different types of soil respond differently to the "raindrops"?

**You can see soil erosion on a bank next to some homes in Argentina.**

# 3.2 Splashing Raindrops on Loose Soil and Grass-Covered Soil
## (An Experiment)

Things YOU will Need:

✓ an adult
✓ 2 narrow boards about 1 meter (1 yd) long and 5 cm (2 in) wide
✓ sharp knife or saw
✓ white blotter paper or heavy paper toweling
✓ tin can lids
✓ tape
✓ tacks
✓ hammer
✓ loose soil
✓ grass-covered soil
✓ rain

Raindrops may splash on loose soil or on grass-covered soil. Do you think there will be a difference in their effect? Form a hypothesis and then do this experiment.

1. Build two splash boards. They will help you see the effects of raindrops splashing on loose soil and grass-covered soil. First, find or make two narrow boards about 1 meter (1 yd) long and 5 cm (2 in) wide.

2. **Ask an adult** to sharpen one end of each board to a point with a knife or saw. Cover one side of each board

# Figure 9

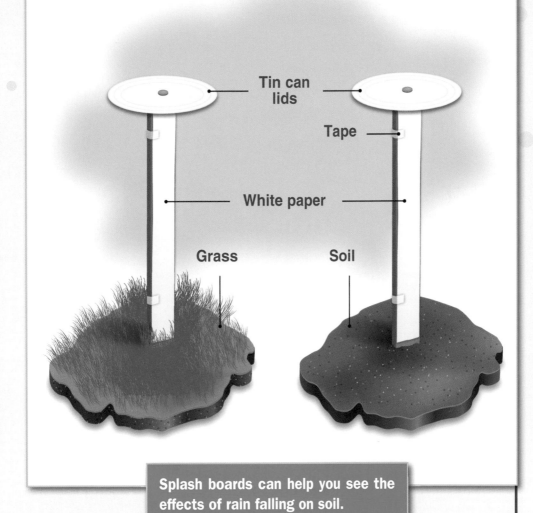

Tin can lids

Tape

White paper

Grass

Soil

Splash boards can help you see the effects of rain falling on soil.

with white blotter paper or heavy paper toweling. Use tacks to hold the paper in place. Tack the lid of a tin can to the top of the flat end of each board, as shown in Figure 9. The lids will keep falling raindrops off the paper.

3. Just before or at the start of a rainstorm, use a hammer to tap one board into loose soil. Tap the other board into grass-covered soil. **Caution: Do not do this experiment during a thunderstorm!**

4. After several minutes in the rain, examine the splash patterns on the two boards. How do they differ?

5. Look at the siding of your house near the foundation after a heavy rainstorm. How can you explain what you see?

What would happen to splashed soil on sloped land?

## Ideas for Science Fair Projects

- Repeat Experiment 3.2 on hillside soil and grass. Does the slope affect the splash pattern?

- Repeat Experiment 3.2 on different kinds of soil. How do the patterns differ?

- Repeat Experiment 3.2 during a windy rainstorm. How does wind affect the splash pattern?

# 3.3 Hillside Agriculture
## (An Experiment)

Things YOU will Need:

✓ pan 7 to 12 cm (3 to 5 in) deep
✓ moist garden soil
✓ very thin stick or plastic knife
✓ water
✓ watering can

**M**uch farming takes place on land that is not level. If such land is plowed, do you think the direction it is plowed will affect the amount of soil that will be lost to water erosion? Form a hypothesis. Then carry out this experiment.

1. Find a pan 7 to 12 cm (3 to 5 in) deep.

2. Make a sloped bank (hillside) from moist garden soil as shown in Figure 10a. Use your hand to pack it firmly in place.

3. Use a very thin stick or plastic knife to make lines in the soil as shown in Figure 10b. The lines represent furrows made by a plow. Make two or three lines that go up and down one side the "hill." Make a similar number across the hill on the other side, as shown.

4. Use a watering can to slowly "rain" evenly across the hillside. Compare the soil erosion from the two types of plowing. Which direction of plowing causes more soil erosion?

Was your hypothesis correct?

If you were a farmer and felt you had to plow a hillside, would you plow up and down or across it?

## Figure 10

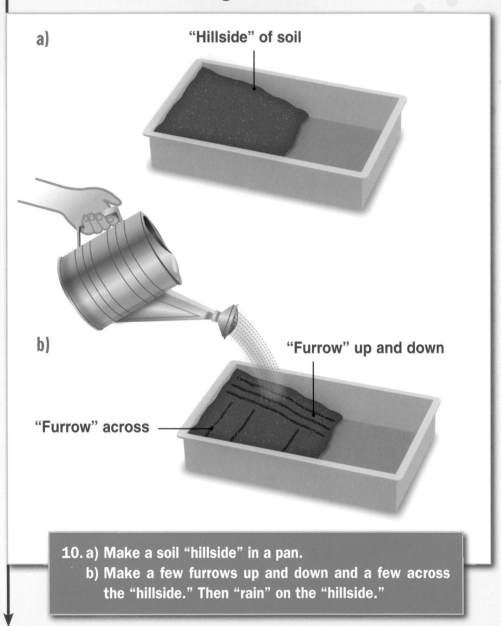

a) "Hillside" of soil

b) "Furrow" up and down

"Furrow" across

10. a) Make a soil "hillside" in a pan.
   b) Make a few furrows up and down and a few across the "hillside." Then "rain" on the "hillside."

# 3.4 Soil Erosion
## (An Experiment)

**Things YOU will Need:**

- ✓ 2 long, narrow, cardboard boxes, such as candy boxes
- ✓ aluminum foil
- ✓ nail
- ✓ moist topsoil or garden soil
- ✓ grass seed
- ✓ water
- ✓ warm, sunlit area
- ✓ wood blocks or bricks
- ✓ 2 shallow plastic containers
- ✓ watering can
- ✓ measuring cup

**F**armers that have to grow crops on steep hillsides often terrace the sloped land. They plant crops on the level parts of the terraces and grass on the slopes (Figure 11a). Why do you think they plant grass on the sloped land? Form a hypothesis. Then do this experiment.

1. Line two long, narrow, cardboard boxes, such as candy boxes, with aluminum foil.

2. Using a nail, punch holes in one end of each box, as shown in Figure 11b. Add equal amounts of moist topsoil or garden soil to each box.

3. Sprinkle grass seed over the soil in one box. Gently work the seeds into the top of the soil. Sprinkle the soil in both

## Figure 11

a)

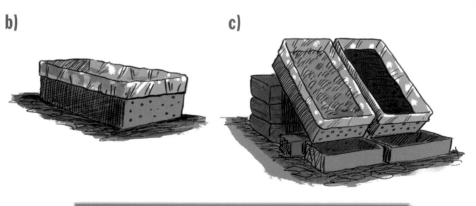

b)                    c)

11. a) Terraced farmland
    b) Box lined with aluminum foil; holes punched through one end
    c) Tilted soils to compare erosion of grassy and bare soil

boxes with water and keep the soils moist but not wet. Place both boxes in a warm, sunlit area.

4. When the grass is growing well, use blocks of wood or bricks to tilt both trays at the same angle.

5. Place a plastic container under the lower end of each tilted box, as shown in Figure 11c.

6. Use a watering can to sprinkle a quart of water over each box of soil. Eroded soil will collect in the lower plastic containers. If very little erosion occurs, sprinkle another quart or two of water onto each box. Is the erosion greater in the seeded or unseeded soil?

Was your hypothesis correct?

Would you expect more erosion on a grassy or a soil-covered slope?

# Idea for a Science Fair Project

Repeat Experiment 3.4, but this time fill both boxes with the same amount of loose, moist, unseeded soil. Tilt one box so that its soil makes a much steeper slope than the other. In which box is there more erosion? Can you explain why? What is the effect of gravity on erosion?

# 3.5 Looking for Local Erosion
## (An Observation)

**Things YOU will Need:**

✓ evidence of erosion near your home

**E**rosion is commonly seen along rivers or at the edge of the ocean where waves batter the shore. But you can probably find erosion near your home no matter where you live.

1. Look outdoors for places where grass has been worn away. Areas along paths or sidewalks are good places to look. Can you find places where soil has eroded, creating dry, miniature riverbeds like the one in the photograph?

2. If you find erosion, ask if you can do something to reduce or eliminate it. What might you do to stop or reduce the erosion?

Soil erosion along a road

# 3.6 Glacial Erosion
## (A Demonstration and an Experiment)

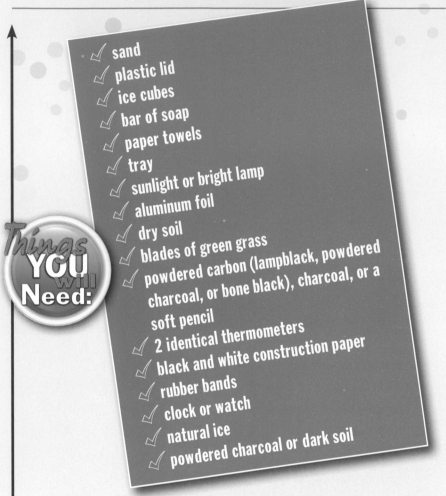

*Things* **YOU** *will* **Need:**

- ✓ sand
- ✓ plastic lid
- ✓ ice cubes
- ✓ bar of soap
- ✓ paper towels
- ✓ tray
- ✓ sunlight or bright lamp
- ✓ aluminum foil
- ✓ dry soil
- ✓ blades of green grass
- ✓ powdered carbon (lampblack, powdered charcoal, or bone black), charcoal, or a soft pencil
- ✓ 2 identical thermometers
- ✓ black and white construction paper
- ✓ rubber bands
- ✓ clock or watch
- ✓ natural ice
- ✓ powdered charcoal or dark soil

Glaciers are huge blocks of ice hundreds of feet thick that cover thousands of square miles of Earth's surface. Although many glaciers are shrinking because of global warming, many still exist and continue to erode Earth's soil.

1. A glacier can change the ground over which it moves. To see how it does this, first, pour a thin layer of sand onto a plastic lid. Then place an ice cube on the sand. The ice represents the glacier; the sand represents the soil that the glacier drags.

2. Place a bar of soap on a paper towel. Rub the sandy side of the ice cube over the bar of soap. The soap represents the ground over which the glacier moves. What does the sand under the ice do to the soap?

When glaciers shrink (recede), they also change the landscape. To see how, go on to step 3.

3. Dip the same ice cube in the sand again. Let the ice cube rest on the soap and melt like a receding glacier. What is left after the ice melts? You have created a miniature moraine. (A moraine is the area of sediment and rocks left by a glacier when it melts.)

4. During droughts, airplanes are sometimes used in glacial regions to spray lampblack (powdered carbon) over the glaciers. To see why, first gather aluminum foil, dry soil, blades of green grass, and powdered carbon (lampblack, powdered charcoal, or bone black). If you don't have any carbon, you can make some by scraping a piece of charcoal or the end of a pencil that has thick, black "lead" (graphite).

5. Place a few identical ice cubes on a tray lined with paper towels. Cover one ice cube with aluminum foil; cover another ice cube with dry soil, another with blades of green grass, another with powdered carbon (lampblack, powdered charcoal, or bone black) or powder from charcoal or pencil "lead" (graphite). Leave one ice cube uncovered to serve as a control.

**6.** Put the tray near a window where sunlight will fall equally on all the ice cubes. Or put them under a bright lamp. Which ice cube melts fastest? Which melts slowest?

**7.** To see why some ice cubes melted faster than others, you will need two identical thermometers. Wrap the bulb end of one thermometer with black construction paper. Wrap the second thermometer with white construction paper. Rubber bands can be used to hold the paper in place, as shown in Figure 12. Set both thermometers side by side in sunlight or under a heat lamp. Watch the thermometers. Which one warms faster? How does the color of the paper affect its ability to absorb solar energy?

**8.** If it is winter, find some natural ice on which the sun shines. Sprinkle one area of the ice with powdered charcoal or dark soil. How do you think the darkened area of ice will compare with the surrounding ice after several hours in the sun? Was your prediction correct?

## Figure 12

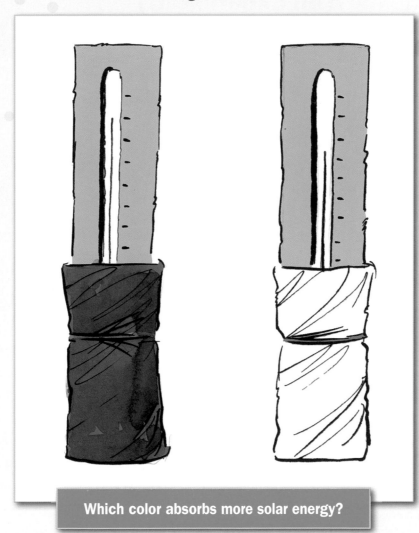

Which color absorbs more solar energy?

# 3.7 Dark Soil, Solar Energy, and Erosion
## (An Experiment)

**Things YOU will Need:**
- ✓ shallow pan or tray
- ✓ damp soil
- ✓ bright sunlight or bright light
- ✓ safety glasses

**W**hen farmers plow the earth, they turn up dark soil. As you know from the previous demonstration, dark soil in the sun will become warmer than lighter matter, such as grass. What do you think will happen to dark, damp soil when it is heated by light? Make a hypothesis. Then do this experiment.

1. Cover a shallow pan or tray with some damp soil.

2. Put the tray in bright sunlight or under a bright light for a day. What happens to the wet soil? What would happen to this soil if it were on a slope and rain fell on it? What would happen if a strong wind blew across this soil? Form a hypothesis about the wind on the dry soil. Then go to step 3.

3. **Put on safety glasses** and go outside. To simulate the effect of wind on dry soil, blow across the soil. What happens to the soil? Did the "wind" cause erosion? Was your hypothesis correct?

# 3.8 River-Caused Erosion
## (A Demonstration)

*Things* **YOU** *will* **Need:**

☑ shovel
☑ soil from a garden or field
☑ hose
☑ outside faucet

**E**ach year rivers carry vast amounts of soil to the oceans. To demonstrate how this happens, you can build a small "mountain" and create a "river" that flows down it. Gravity is the force that moves water along rivers and streams whether the slope is steep or slight.

1. Obtain permission to use a shovel to build a pile of soil dug from a garden or field. Make the pile two or three feet high.

2. Connect a garden hose to an outside faucet. Hold the end of the hose near the top of your "mountain," as shown in Figure 13. Turn on the faucet so that water flows slowly onto a point on or near the top of your mountain.

3. Notice how the water creates a "river" that flows down the mountain. Do you see any tiny waterfalls? Do you see pebbles collecting along the riverbanks?

4. At the bottom of the mountain, the water flows more slowly. Can you explain why?

# Figure 13

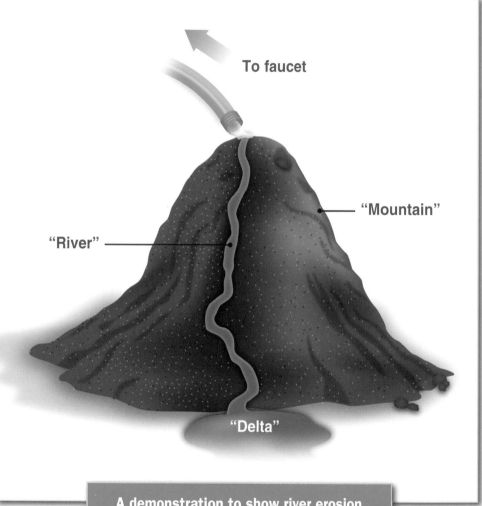

To faucet

"Mountain"

"River"

"Delta"

**A demonstration to show river erosion**

5. Notice a delta (a fan-shaped area of deposited soil) forming at the mouth of the river. This corresponds to deltas that form where a river enters an ocean or lake.

6. Build a dam with more soil to block the river at some point along its course. A "reservoir" or "lake" will form behind the dam. Water flowing over a real dam could be used to generate electricity without adding carbon dioxide to the atmosphere—but the reservoir or lake could significantly damage the land it covers.

## Idea for a Science Fair Project

Newly formed (young) mountains usually have sharp peaks. Design and carry out an experiment to show what happens as a young mountain ages.

# 3.9 Wind Erosion
## (An Experiment)

**Things YOU will Need:**
- safety glasses
- cardboard box about 30 cm (12 in) wide and high, 45 cm (18 in) long
- basement, garage, or outdoor area
- small table (optional)
- dry sand
- hair dryer or small fan
- wet sand

**D**o you think wet soil or dry soil will erode more readily when struck by wind? Form a hypothesis and then do this experiment.

1. Remove the top and one end of a cardboard box as shown in Figure 14. Take the box to a basement, garage, or outdoors. Put it on a small table, the floor, or the ground.

2. Place a small pile of dry sand near the open end of the box.

3. **Put on safety glasses.** Then use a hair dryer or small fan to create wind. Let the wind blow across the sand for several minutes. Can wind cause soil erosion?

4. Repeat the experiment, but this time use wet sand. How does the erosion of wet sand compare with the erosion of dry sand? Was your hypothesis correct?

Save the materials used in this experiment for the next experiment.

Figure 14

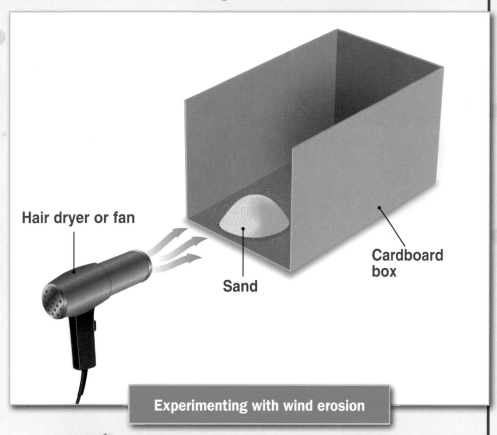

**Hair dryer or fan**

**Sand**

**Cardboard box**

Experimenting with wind erosion

## Idea for a Science Fair Project

Design and do experiments to see which type or types of dry and wet soil are most resistant to wind erosion. You might try sand, garden soil, potting soil, clay soil, and others.

Wind can change rock to soil. These rock statues in Utah's Goblin Valley State Park were carved by the wind. The rock particles carried off by the wind became part of Earth's soil.

# 3.10 Reducing Wind Erosion
## (A Demonstration)

**P**lanting hedgerows (trees and bushes) next to fields where crops are grown is one way to reduce wind erosion. To see why this reduces erosion, you can repeat Experiment 3.9, but with a "hedgerow."

**1.** Prepare a cardboard box and a pile of dry sand as you did before (see Figure 14). Take the box to a basement, garage, or outdoors. Put it on a small table, the floor, or the ground.

**2. Put on safety glasses.** You will use a hair dryer or small fan to create wind, as you did in Experiment 3.9. But this time, hold a piece of cardboard, such as the one you removed from the end of the box, between the hair dryer and the sand. The cardboard represents a hedgerow planted to protect the soil.

**3.** Turn on the hair dryer to create wind. Let the wind blow on the hedgerow for several minutes. How does the hedgerow reduce wind erosion?

SOIL

## Idea for a Science Fair Project

You may have seen snow fences along highways. The fences partially block the wind, causing wind-borne particles to fall. This keeps wind-blown snow off roads. Perhaps similar fences can be used to prevent soil from blowing away. Do an experiment to test this idea. You can make miniature "snow fences" from wooden coffee stirrers or craft sticks.

## The Great Dust Storm

In May of 1934, following a prolonged drought, a wind-driven storm created a dust cloud three miles high that covered more than a million square miles. It stretched from Canada to Texas and from Montana to Ohio. The wind carried 300 million tons of soil 1,500 miles, dropping dust on ships 300 miles east of the Atlantic coast of the United States. And more dust storms followed. There were 300 reported in North Dakota during an eight-month period. Oklahoma suffered through 102 such storms in a single year.

The so-called Dust Bowl of the 1930s was caused by poor farming methods followed by a prolonged drought. During the 1920s, tractors were used to plow up the native grasslands of the Great Plains in order to plant wheat. The acreage of wheat fields doubled in less than a decade, replacing prairie sod with dry soil that blew away when high winds moved across it.

Poor farming methods and drought created the Dust Bowl in the 1930s.

# Improving Earth's Soil

Topsoil, which took millions of years to reach an average depth of 15 cm (6 in), is eroding. But there are ways we can help preserve topsoil. Farmers can plant cover crops and use non-tillage farming, for example. Keeping soil covered with vegetation keeps soil in place and prevents erosion. The decomposing vegetation increases the soil's organic matter and nutrients. Such farming reduces the use of heavy machinery and thereby reduces soil compaction.

Healthy soil requires water, so we should do all we can to conserve it. One way to do this is to increase the production of crops that require less water.

Growing wheat rather than rice, a crop that requires lots of water, will reduce water needs. And there are new methods to irrigate soil, such as underground drip irrigation.

Global warming threatens food production because of changes in climate. Regions where soils had plenty of water are now becoming drier. Soils in other areas are subject to flooding. To combat global warming, we need to reduce atmospheric carbon dioxide. To reach this goal, our sources of energy must change. Fossil fuels, which all emit carbon dioxide, must be replaced by renewable energy sources such as wind, solar, and geothermal.

Planting trees will hold soil in place and prevent it from eroding. That soil will hold water that might otherwise run off and cause flooding. Trees, like all green plants, absorb carbon dioxide and release oxygen, so another benefit will be a reduction in global warming.

# 3.11 Waves and Beach Erosion
## (A Demonstration)

**Things YOU will Need:**

- ✓ ruler
- ✓ pan 7 to 12 cm (3 to 5 in) deep
- ✓ moist garden soil
- ✓ water
- ✓ ruler
- ✓ wood block

**B**eaches, such as those along the shore of Cape Cod, Massachusetts, are struck each year by giant waves generated by storm winds. The banks behind these beaches lose an average of three feet of soil each year as a result of erosion caused by wind and waves. To see how this happens, you can do a simulation.

1. Find a pan 7 to 12 cm (3 to 5 in) deep.

2. Make a sloped "beach bank" from moist garden soil, as shown in Figure 15a. Use your hand to pack it firmly in place.

3. Add water to the pan until it is about 3 cm (1 in) deep.

4. Place a block of wood at the end of the pan opposite the shore. You can use the block to generate waves.

5. Make small waves by gently moving the block back and forth. These waves, associated with calm seas, do little damage to the beach bank.

# Figure 15

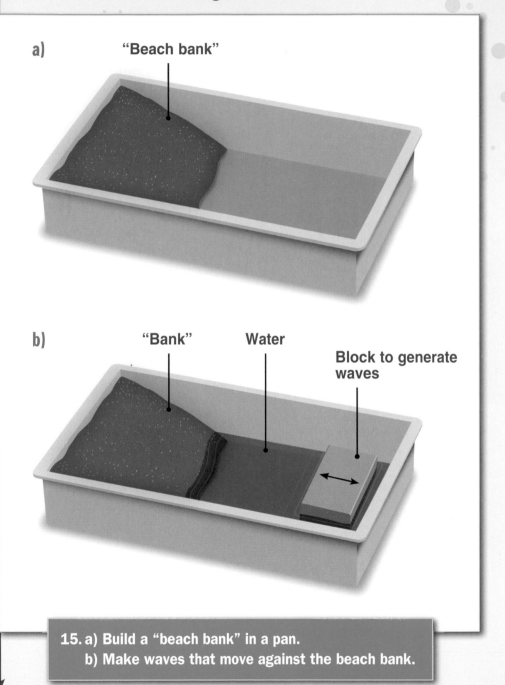

a) "Beach bank"

b) "Bank"    Water

Block to generate waves

15. a) Build a "beach bank" in a pan.
    b) Make waves that move against the beach bank.

**6.** Make larger "storm waves" by moving the block up and down. Continue making storm waves for several minutes. What happens to the beach bank?

Ocean waves have carved soil from the bank of this Cape Cod beach.

# Conserving Soil

**W**ind and water erosion carry away topsoil from American farmland at an annual rate of approximately 30 tons per hectare (12 tons per acre). The result is less healthy soil. There are a number of reasons for the decrease in healthy soil. One reason is poor farming methods. Some farmers are more interested in making short-term profits than in maintaining healthy soil.

Another cause of soil erosion is deforestation. Trees and shrubs hold soil together and absorb huge quantities of water. The cutting of forests can result in such spectacular erosion as landslides and avalanches. This is particularly true on sloped land where water can quickly carry soil away. More than half the topsoil in the United States has been lost because of farming methods and deforestation.

In some parts of the world, especially South America, rain forests have been destroyed by the "slash-and-burn" method to make more farmland. After this land is farmed and loses its fertility, more of the rain forest is cut down and the process is repeated. Trees cannot grow back on the cultivated land because most of the soil's nutrients have been removed by the intense farming methods. The problem is compounded by the fact that rain forests are rich in chlorophyll, the green pigment in leaves. These forests produce vast amounts of oxygen and remove similar amounts of carbon dioxide through photosynthesis. Removing such forests leaves large quantities of carbon dioxide in the atmosphere. Increasing the atmospheric concentration of carbon dioxide accelerates global warming.

Farmland is also lost every year to salinization—the accumulation of salts in the soil that make farming impossible because most plants cannot tolerate high salt concentrations.

Additional farmland used for pasture becomes unproductive every year as a result of overgrazing. As the plants that promote animal growth and health disappear, they are replaced by weeds and plants that are less beneficial to the animals. Overgrazing tends to compact the soil. Animals grazing in the same area too long trample the soil, making it very hard. You will see the effects of compaction in a later experiment.

You have already seen how wind and water can cause soil erosion, but let's look at these other factors affecting soil in more detail.

## Salinization and Its Causes

Salt enters the soil naturally when rock particles dissolve in groundwater. When groundwater is less than 3 meters (10 ft) from the surface in clay-rich soils, it rises to the surface by capillary action. Once there, it evaporates, leaving salt on the soil.

Another natural source is rainwater, which also contains small quantities of dissolved salt. In fact, tiny salt particles often serve as centers on which water vapor collects to form raindrops.

The major cause of salty soil is irrigation. When crops are irrigated, especially in arid regions, much of the water evaporates, leaving salt behind on the soil. Of course, some of the salt is removed when plants absorb it.

A rising water table can carry salt to the upper soil, causing salinization. The water table may rise when excess irrigation water percolates into the soil. Other causes include water leaking into the ground from nearby reservoirs, rivers, or irrigation ditches.

A *falling* water table near the ocean can also cause salinization. When the underground water table drops below the ocean level, salty ocean water will move into the groundwater.

The Aswan Dam in Egypt was built to control the flooding of the

**Only the green areas in this aerial photograph are irrigated.**

Nile River. This river is the source of irrigation water for farmland below the dam. However, the dam has led to a lower water table near the sea into which the river empties. As a result, salt water from the ocean has seeped into farmland.

A number of ancient civilizations in the Middle East were destroyed as their irrigated land became increasingly salty. Ur and Uruk, old cities in Iraq, diminished in population as the salt concentration in their soil grew.

# 4.1 A Source of Salt
## (An Experiment)

✓ small, black, plastic tray such as the kind in which some frozen meals are sold
✓ tap water
✓ sunlight or heat lamp (optional)

**D**o you think salt can be detected in tap water? Form a hypothesis. Then do this experiment.

1. Find a small, black, plastic tray such as the kind in which some frozen meals are sold.

2. Cover the bottom of the tray with tap water about 3 cm (1 in) deep.

3. Place the tray in bright sunlight, under a heat lamp, or, if you are willing to wait for several days, in a warm place where it will not be disturbed.

4. After the water has evaporated, is there any evidence that there was salt dissolved in the tap water? If so, what is the evidence?

## Partial Solutions to Salinization

How can soil salinization problems be addressed?

Salt-tolerant plants, such as saltwater cordgrass and switchgrass, will grow in salty soil. They grow naturally along the edges of salt-marsh streams.

**Ideas for Science Fair Projects**

- Do experiments to see if salt can be detected in rainwater.
- Do experiments to see if salt can be detected in bottled water.
- Do experiments to see if salt can be detected in lake or pond water.
- Ordinary salt is sodium chloride (NaCl). How can you test to see if the white solid is sodium chloride? What other salts might be present?

Such plants can store salt in their cells, so one way to remove excess salt from soil is to grow these plants. When the plants are harvested, salt is removed from the soil.

Salinization can be slowed by adding water faster than it can evaporate or be absorbed by plants. The excess water moves through the soil, carrying salt to the nearest river or sea. This approach is expensive because it uses large quantities of valuable irrigation water. And, unfortunately, the water flowing into the river may make the water so salty that it is unfit for human consumption or aquatic life. Downstream communities that obtain their water from such a river will have to find another source or build a desalinization plant, which is very expensive.

Drip irrigation systems that deliver water directly to plant roots reduce the amount of water needed because far less water evaporates. In arid Israel, where water is extremely scarce, drip irrigation is used. It reduces water lost to evaporation by more than 80 percent.

## Clearing Rain Forests: Soil Effects

Rain forests are filled with thriving plant life. However, the soils of these forests lack high concentrations of nutrients. The plants absorb the nutrients very rapidly, so the nutrients are found in the plants rather than the soil. When such forests are cleared, the remaining soil is exposed to heavy rains that carry the soil away because there is no vegetation to hold it.

## Desertification

As populations grow in arid parts of the world, the soil becomes farmed, grazed, and deforested faster than it can recover. As a result, nothing is left to hold the soil in place. The limited amount of topsoil erodes, leaving a desert. The people then move on, repeating the process in another arid region.

## Desertification, Drought, and Famine

Droughts—severely reduced rainfall—are part of the natural weather cycle. In 1985, people in Ethiopia were starving. Drought and war had resulted in a major reduction in crops. The soil had dried up and plants had died because groundwater levels dropped far below their roots. When the rains did come in the fall, millions of tons of topsoil were carried away as water ran off into rivers.

# Responding to Desertification

Planting salt-tolerant trees and shrubs is probably the best way to improve arid, salty soil. Trees hold the soil in place and act as wind screens, reducing soil loss to wind erosion. Trees such as Prosopis, a legume tree, can grow in arid saline soil and produce pods that can be used as animal food. Trees provide shade, which reduces evaporation, allowing salt-tolerant crops to grow. Such methods make it possible to reclaim some desert soil, but the process takes decades.

# Reducing Erosion, Conserving Soil

One way to reduce erosion is to plant grass. Many varieties of grass will grow not only on lawns and pastures but on open prairies, mountainsides, marshes, steep slopes, or even sand dunes. The roots of grasses help hold soil in place. They provide a cover for soil that reduces erosion from wind and rain.

All grasses have narrow leaves, parallel leaf veins, small flowers, hollow, jointed, round stems, and a sheath around the stem at the base of each leaf. If you have a lawn, you know that grasses are very resilient. They can survive and flourish after being cut to the ground. They continue to grow even after being subjected to mowing, stomping, burning, and grazing.

This grass growing on sand dunes holds the soil in place and helps to reduce erosion.

Unlike most plants, grasses grow from the base of their stems, not the tips. If the leaf or shoot is cut or damaged, it grows back. Also, grasses spread horizontally, forming a dense blanket not easily penetrated by other plants. Because their pollen is carried by the wind, grasses can spread over wide areas.

## Farming Methods

Many U.S. farms strive for maximum output from minimum input in order to maximize profits. They often produce a single crop, such as corn or wheat. To replace the nutrients removed by the crop, they add fertilizers that contain nitrogen, phosphorus, and potassium. Often they add more chemicals than are needed. The excess may be carried away by rain or irrigation water to nearby rivers, contaminating the water and promoting the growth of algae.

The use of pesticides and herbicides, especially in excess, can contaminate the food crop being grown as well as water that drains from the soil into rivers and streams.

Farms growing livestock are often more like factories than farms. Animals are crowded into limited space and fed grains to make them grow as rapidly as possible. They are soon slaughtered and replaced with a new "crop." Such methods are sometimes characterized as conveyor-belt farming.

Organic (green) farmers do not use synthetic pesticides, herbicides, or inorganic fertilizers. A century ago all farms used organic methods because chemical fertilizers were expensive or unavailable and pesticides were unknown. The following methods used in organic farming are becoming more common as advocates of a greener world make people aware of the world's diminishing topsoil.

Rather than using inorganic chemical fertilizers, organic farmers spread organic matter such as compost or manure on their fields. This method adds nutrients to the soil and improves conditions for crops and soil-forming organisms such as earthworms.

Often, a cover crop is grown in the fall. Cover crops, such as rye grass or clover, are crops that are not harvested. Farmers plant the cover crop seeds after their main crops are harvested in the fall. The cover crop grows, and then in the spring it is plowed back into the soil. It adds organic matter and increases topsoil. Then the soil is ready for new crops. While growing, a cover crop holds soil in place, preventing erosion. An organic farmer can make as much money as any other farmer because his or her operating costs are less. He or she doesn't spend money on synthetic fertilizers and pesticides.

Crops that add nitrogen to the soil, such as legumes, are rotated from one season to the next with crops that take up nitrogen, such as corn. As a result, nutrients that are removed by one crop are replaced by another. Crop rotation has been used by European farmers to maintain soil fertility for centuries.

Many organic farmers use no-till farming on at least some of their land. They keep the soil covered with vegetation (remains of the previous crop) to keep soil in place and prevent erosion. As the vegetation decomposes, it adds organic matter and nutrients to the soil. Instead of tilling the soil, the farmer plants the next crop by drilling holes into which seeds are dropped. The roots of the previous crop keep the soil in place. No-till farming requires less water and less energy from both the farmer and his machinery. Also, such farming reduces soil compaction by heavy machinery.

# 4.2 Compacted Soil
## (An Experiment)

**Things YOU will Need:**

- ✓ 2 small containers, such as 6-ounce plastic yogurt cups or paper cups
- ✓ garden soil
- ✓ medicine cup or vial
- ✓ water

In a pasture, animals may compact (press together) the soil by repeatedly walking on it. In a field where crops are growing, the wheels of heavy machinery, such as tractors, may compact the soil. While plowing loosens the upper few inches of soil, the weight of plows and tractors tends to compact deeper soil. Do you think compacted soil will behave differently than regular loose soil? If you do, how do you think it will differ? Form a hypothesis. Then do this experiment.

**1.** Nearly fill two small containers, such as 6-ounce plastic yogurt cups or paper cups, with garden soil.

**2.** Use your fingers to thoroughly compact (press together) the soil in one cup. Leave the soil loose in the other cup.

**3.** Fill a medicine cup or vial with water. Pour the water onto the compacted soil. Pour an equal amount of water onto the loose soil. What do you observe? Was your hypothesis correct?

What is the effect of compacted soil on percolation? What might be the effect of compacted soil on erosion? On plant growth?

## Idea for a Science Fair Project

Design an experiment to measure the degree of soil compaction.

## Compacted Soil

When soil is compacted by grazing animals, machinery, or other forces, it squeezes soil particles together, reducing the spaces between them. This makes it more difficult for water and air to reach the roots of plants and for roots to penetrate through the soil as they grow. Plant roots absorb most of a plant's water, and the roots use oxygen from air to carry on respiration. When rain or irrigation water falls on compacted soil, it is similar to water falling on pavement; much of the water runs off. It carries soil particles with it, causing erosion.

To reduce soil compaction, farmers may add organic matter such as manure and other organic waste to the soil. They may also adopt no-till cultivation, so that less machinery rolls over the soil.

Compacted soil resulting from overgrazing can lead to desertification. However, the added manure from the grazing animals may enrich the soil. A prolonged period during which the land remains fallow (unplanted with crops or without grazing animals) can often restore overgrazed land. The U.S. government used this simple method to restore some overgrazed federal rangeland. Unfortunately, few countries have allowed overgrazed land to remain fallow long enough to avoid desertification.

# 4.3 Composting
## (An Activity)

Things
YOU will
Need:

✓ composting ingredients such as grass, soil, and food scraps
✓ composting bin or a plastic trash can with holes drilled in its side, or fence wire
✓ shovel

Believe it or not, you can make good, rich, garden soil. You can make it by creating a compost pile from matter that you might otherwise throw away. Composting is an inexpensive, greener way to create good soil. Worms and decomposing microorganisms will change the matter into garden soil.

Composting will also reduce the amount of organic waste you discard, helping to slow the growth of your local landfill. Moist compost will reduce the need to water your garden, helping to conserve water. It will also help you avoid chemical fertilizers, which will prevent contamination of groundwater. And growing more plants will help to remove carbon dioxide, a greenhouse gas, from the air.

Composting ingredients can be classified as greens and browns. Greens are fresh materials such as grass clippings and food scraps (not meats, fats, or oils). Browns are dry matter such as soil, leaves, dead grass, and wood chips.

# Figure 16

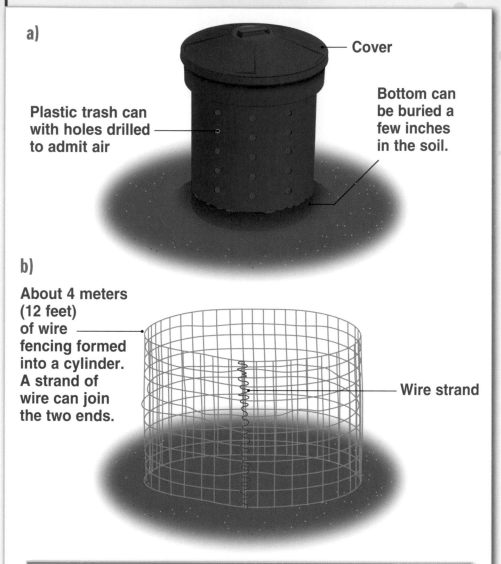

a)

Cover

Plastic trash can with holes drilled to admit air

Bottom can be buried a few inches in the soil.

b)

About 4 meters (12 feet) of wire fencing formed into a cylinder. A strand of wire can join the two ends.

Wire strand

16. a) An old plastic trash can with holes drilled in its side can serve as a bin. Cut off the bottom and bury several inches of the base of the can in soil.

b) Fence wire with 2 inch x 4 inch (or smaller) openings can be made into a cylindrical bin to hold composting matter.

**This compost pile can provide a greener way to make good, fertile soil.**

**1.** To start a compost pile, collect as many greens and browns as possible. Place them in a pile or in a bin. (See Figure 16 for two ways to make a composting bin.) Some communities sell manufactured composting bins at reduced prices.

**2.** Keep the compost moist but not wet. To speed the process, chop the ingredients into small pieces. This increases their surface area, providing more contact between ingredients and the organisms that act on them.

**3.** Mix the pile occasionally by turning and stirring the ingredients with a shovel. This will increase exposure to air and the action of aerobic bacteria.

# You Can Help Conserve Soil and Create a Greener World

Have you ever considered a career in agriculture? Although farming is a very worthwhile career and essential to human survival, farming is not the only career associated with agriculture. You might become a soil analyst, which would involve testing soils and deciding the best ways to use and conserve them. Or you might become an agronomist. By knowing the science of soil management and crop production, you could advise farmers, horticulturists, and home gardeners how best to proceed in their work.

As a county agricultural agent, you could provide valuable information to people involved in all kinds of agricultural work—dairy farming, truck farming, greenhouse agriculture, orchards, hydroponic gardening, and so on.

These occupations, and others related to agriculture, would require at least a bachelor's degree from a college or university that would allow you to major in some aspect of agriculture.

As a college student majoring in environmental studies, you might consider a career as a hydrologist. Hydrologists study water, both above and below the soil. They can offer ways to reduce and control soil erosion, control floods, and advise farmers about irrigation.

Anyone involved in agriculture has one eye on the weather. As a meteorologist (one who studies and predicts weather), you might provide weather reports that would help farmers and others plan their work. You might also investigate ways to seed clouds to produce rain in areas suffering from droughts. To become a meteorologist, you would have to study physics and chemistry in college.

## Green Tips: What You Can Do to Help Conserve Soil

A college education is not needed to help conserve soil. Here are some things you can do right now.

- Make your own soil by establishing a compost pile or bin. You can use that soil to make or add to soil for a garden.

- In 2009, First Lady Michelle Obama used part of the White House grounds to start an organic vegetable garden. You can follow her example by planting and caring for a vegetable garden of your own. Be sure your garden is on level ground, terraced, or enclosed by logs or large lumber so that the soil cannot erode.

- If you have a lawn, don't put short grass clippings in the trash. Leave them on the lawn. They serve as a natural mulch and fertilizer for the soil. Long grass clippings can be added to your compost.

- In coastal areas, never walk or drive on dune grass. Dune grass traps sand and holds beach soil in place.

- If you live near a pond or stream, do not remove natural groundcover, such as trees and bushes. They help to prevent bank erosion. The eroded soil can smother aquatic plants, clog the gills of fish, and reduce the light reaching underwater plants.

- Use paving materials that are permeable so that rainwater can enter the soil. Bricks, flat stones, crushed stones, and deck boards with gaps between them allow water to reach soil. Be sure to keep decking above the ground to avoid rotting.

- Where impermeable surfaces exist, divert rain runoff onto grass or other ground cover so that it can enter the soil.

- Where a new structure is being built, ask the builder to leave as much of the original vegetation as possible. Be sure hay bales are in place around the building site to contain soil and avoid erosion.

- Do not use chemical fertilizers on lawns. They can contaminate the underlying soil and groundwater.

- Plant sloped ground with grass and other vegetation to prevent soil erosion.

- If your family has a motor boat, avoid making large wakes near shore. These wakes (waves) can cause shore erosion.

- Plant trees and bushes. They help hold soil in place and reduce wind erosion. But do not plant trees near walks, pools, or septic leach fields. Their roots can crack or raise concrete or macadam and block septic drains.

- Establish a Web site to educate people about living green and offering ideas on how to do so by conserving soil.

# Appendix:
# Science Supply Companies

**Arbor Scientific**
P.O. Box 2750
Ann Arbor, MI 48106-2750
(800) 367-6695
www.arborsci.com

**Carolina Biological Supply Co.**
2700 York Road
Burlington, NC 27215-3398
(800) 334-5551
http://www.carolina.com

**Connecticut Valley Biological
    Supply Co., Inc.**
82 Valley Road, Box 326
Southampton, MA 01073
(800) 628-7748
http://www.ctvalleybio.com/

**Delta Education**
P.O. Box 3000
80 Northwest Blvd
Nashua, NH 03061-3000
(800) 258-1302
customerservice@delta-
    education.com

**Edmund Scientific's Scientifics**
60 Pearce Avenue
Tonawanda, NY 14150-6711
(800) 728-6999
http://www.scientificsonline.com

**Educational Innovations, Inc.**
362 Main Avenue
Norwalk, CT 06851
(888) 912-7474
http://www.teachersource.com

**Fisher Science Education**
4500 Turnberry Drive
Hanover Park, IL 60133
(800) 955-1177
http://www.fishersci.com/

**Frey Scientific**
100 Paragon Parkway
Mansfield, OH 44903
(800) 225-3739
http://www.freyscientific.com/

**Nasco-Fort Atkinson**
P.O. Box 901
Fort Atkinson, WI 53538-0901
(800) 558-9595
http://www.enasco.com/science/

**Nasco-Modesto**
P.O. Box 3837
Modesto, CA 95352-3837
(800) 558-9595
http://www.enasco.com/science/

**Sargent-Welch/VWR Scientific**
P.O. Box 5229
Buffalo Grove, IL 60089-5229
(800) SAR-GENT
http://www.SargentWelch.com

**Science Kit & Boreal Laboratories**
777 East Park Drive
P.O. Box 5003
Tonawanda, NY 14150
(800) 828-7777
http://sciencekit.com

**Wards Natural Science
    Establishment**
P.O. Box 92912
Rochester, NY 14692-9012
(800) 962-2660
http://www.wardsci.com/

# Glossary

**acid-base indicators**—Substances that change color in different concentrations of hydrogen ions.

**acid rain**—Rain that has a pH less than 5. It is caused by gases such as sulfur dioxide and nitrogen dioxide that dissolve in raindrops to form weak solutions of sulfuric and nitric acid.

**acids**—Chemicals that release hydrogen ions ($H^+$) in water.

**aquifer**—Soil or rocks where water saturates (fills) the spaces between the rocks and soil particles.

**bases**—Chemicals that form hydroxide ions ($OH^-$) in water.

**capillarity**—The tendency of liquids such as water to "climb up" narrow tubes and spaces such as those between soil particles.

**clay**—Soil particles that are less than 0.002 millimeters in diameter.

**compacted soil**—Soil that has been pressed together, usually by animals or farm machinery.

**composting**—Making soil from food scraps, grass, wood chips, and other organic matter.

**condensation**—The change of a gas, such as water vapor, to a liquid, such as water.

**desertification**—The conversion of topsoil to sandy desert soil after overcultivation, overgrazing, or deforestation.

**erosion**—The wearing down, loosening, and movement of soil by water, wind, gravity, trampling, or glaciers.

**evaporation**—The change of a liquid to a gas.

**germination**—The emergence of a baby plant from a seed.

**global warming**—The slow warming of Earth's atmosphere because of greenhouse gases such as carbon dioxide that reflect heat back to Earth.

**gravel**—Particles found in soil that are larger than 2.0 millimeters.

**hydroponics**—Growing plants in a medium other than soil, such as water. Nutrients needed for the plants to grow must be added to the medium.

**loam**—A mixture of soil particles, 20 percent of which are clay, 40 percent sand, and 40 percent silt. Loam is rich in organic matter and is an excellent soil for growing most crops.

**percolation**—The passage of water through soil. Soils that allow percolation are said to be permeable.

**permeability**—The ability of a soil to allow water to pass through it.

**pH**—A measure of the concentration of hydrogen ions. Substances with a pH less than 7 are acidic; substances with a pH greater than 7 are basic; substances with a pH of 7 are neutral.

**salinization**—The accumulation of salt in soil.

**sand**—Soil particles that range in size from 0.06 to 2.0 millimeters.

**silt**—Soil particles that are 0.002 to 0.06 millimeters in diameter.

**soil**—A mixture of tiny pieces of rock and decaying or decayed organic matter (dead plants and animals) as well as air and water.

**soot**—Small particles of carbon.

**subsoils**—The layers of soil between topsoil and bedrock.

**tectonic plates**—The separate plates that make up Earth's crust. The plates "float" on Earth's mantle.

**terminal velocity**—The constant velocity of a falling object when the force of gravity is balanced by a resisting force such as air friction or water pressure.

**terraced land**—Land that consists of strips of flat land across hillsides. Land is often terraced to reduce soil erosion.

**topsoil**—The dark, top layer of soil rich in organic matter and nutrients.

**water table**—The top of an aquifer.

**weathering**—The breaking of rocks into small particles that become part of the soil. Weathering may be caused by freezing, wind, acid rain, expansion due to temperature changes, and other weather events.

# Further Reading

## Books

Bardhan-Quallen, Sudipta. *Championship Science Fair Projects: 100 Sure-to-Win Experiments.* New York: Sterling, 2007.

Gifford, Clive. *Weathering and Erosion.* North Mankato, Minn.: Smart Apple Media, 2006.

Hyde, Natalie. *Micro Life in Soil.* New York: Crabtree Publishing Company, 2010.

McKay, Kim, and Jenny Bonnin. *True Green: 100 Everyday Ways You Can Contribute to a Healthier Planet.* Washington, D.C.: National Geographic Society, 2008.

Redlin, Janice L., editor. *Land Abuse and Soil Erosion.* New York: Weigl Publishers, Inc., 2006.

Rhadigan, Joe, and Rain Newcomb. *Prize-Winning Science Fair Projects for Curious Kids.* New York: Lark Books, 2006.

Woods, Michael, and Mary B. Woods. *Mud Flows and Landslides.* Minneapolis: Lerner Publications Company, 2007.

## Internet Addresses

**Earth Day**
**<http://www.earthday.org>**

**NASA. Soil Science Education Homepage.**
**<http://soil.gsfc.nasa.gov/>**

# Index